150 BEST NEW COTTAGE AND CABIN IDEAS

150 BEST NEW COTTAGE AND CABIN IDEAS

FRANCESC ZAMORA MOLA

HARPER
DESIGN

An Imprint of HarperCollinsPublishers

First published in 2020 by
Harper Design
An Imprint of *HarperCollins*Publishers
195 Broadway
New York, NY 10007
Tel.: (212) 207-7000
Fax: (855) 746-6023
harperdesign@harpercollins.com
www.hc.com

Distributed throughout the world by
*HarperCollins*Publishers
195 Broadway
New York, NY 10007

Editorial coordinator: Claudia Martínez Alonso
Art director: Mireia Casanovas Soley
Editor and texts: Francesc Zamora Mola
Layout: Cristina Simó Perales

ISBN 978-0-06-299514-8

Library of Congress Control Number: 2020000623

Printed in Singapore
First printing, 2020

CONTENTS

INTRODUCTION

Gone are the days when retreats out in the wild were mainly summer escape hideaways. Today's cottages and cabins are for all-season use, making them the delight of hikers, explorers, and urbanites searching for peace of mind. They are practical, comfortable, and built to withstand the harsh climates in the high mountains or the rugged coast. Some are basic and sparsely fitted shelters; others are unique "glamping" (glamorous camping) retreats with all the comforts of the home or, better yet, with the amenities of a luxury hotel including hot tub, sauna, and Wi-Fi.

The glamping concept is gaining strength, attracting nature lovers unwilling to give up comfort, and promising an experience of pure enjoyment and relaxation in the context of a distinctive sustainable design. Clearly, the idea of escaping to remote locations to reconnect with nature has expanded its experiential boundaries, but the traditional log cabin, the mountain cottage, or the beach hut prevail as the timeless structures that celebrate nature, sensibly integrated into their surroundings.

Cabin design mostly remains modest in form and function, with an architecture that is strongly rooted in the history and cultural heritage of a place. Cottage and cabin design often takes cues from the vernacular architecture, adopting forms and styles that are reminiscent of rural construction, such as farmhouses, barns, sheds, and stables.

Needless to say, contemporary design takes these traditional forms to another level, adapting them to new standards of habitability, using modern technology and new materials, while enhancing the connection between indoor and outdoor spaces.

Glass and wood take center stage as the predominant materials used inside and out. Generous fenestration opens interior spaces to the daylight and the views. Simple constructions are wrapped in wood board and batten or shingles, left untreated to be weathered by the sunlight, rain, and wind until they turn the tones of the surrounding landscape. Inside, wood brings warm comfort and rustic appeal to modern interiors. Concrete floors extend throughout, echoing the bluish-gray color of granite outcroppings outside.

It is through this aesthetic pursuit inspired by natural forms and colors and vernacular architecture that contemporary design for cottages and cabins highlights construction principles based on sustainability. Such principles were already implanted in vernacular architecture through the consideration of factors including geographical, topographical, climatic, as well as cultural and historic. Sustainable principles and the designs they generate evolve to reflect the use of materials and technology that is inherently linked to a place and time.

Cottages and cabins celebrate the spirit of the place, a place for the enjoyment of the awe-inspiring natural world. There, surrounded by woods and wildlife, and refreshed by the cool mountain air, one is connected to nature and disconnected from urban life.

Lost Whiskey
Concrete Cabin

160 sq ft

GreenSpur

Marshall, Virginia, United States

© Mitch Allen Photography

The Lost Whiskey Club is a members' only speakeasy on top of a mountain. The club is about reconnecting to the lost art of shelter, gather, and nature. Located only an hour away from downtown DC and bordering two state parks and the Appalachian Trail, the club also includes several cabins, a farmhouse, and a mobile whiskey bar. The Lost Whiskey Concrete Cabin is off-grid when it comes to power and water supply. It is made of precast concrete panels, reclaimed wood, and steel, expressing a rustic yet modern aesthetic. The generous fenestration offers views of the formidable natural surroundings, while a deck with a fire pit, a hot tub, and a hammock make for a relaxed stay in the wilderness.

001

Outdoor spaces are an integral part of cabin design. Whether these spaces are for eating, playing, or relaxing, they offer quality time away from the busy urban environment and improve human connection with nature.

The interior of the Lost Whiskey Concrete Cabin is a single room with a murphy bed, a sitting area around a wood-burning stove, and a bathroom with a shower and composite toilet.

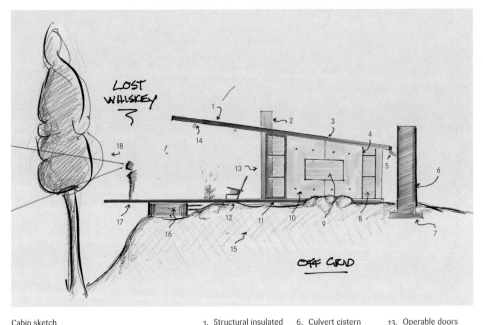

Cabin sketch

1. Structural insulated
   panels (SIPs)
2. Steel chimney
3. Solar panels
4. Steel windows
5. Rainwater
   collection

6. Culvert cistern
7. Concrete footing
8. Shower/Bathroom
9. Kitchen window
10. Concrete panels
11. Steel chassis
12. Drinking chair

13. Operable doors
14. LED puck lights
15. Rock outcropping
16. Wood-fired hot tub
17. Hammock over cliff
    into trees
18. Views

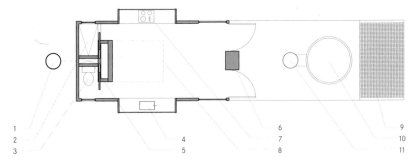

Floor plan

1. Cistern
2. Shower
3. Composting toilet
4. Sink
5. Battery storage
6. Wood burning stove

7. Propane cooktop
8. Murphy bed/table
9. Hammock net
10. Dutch net
11. Fire pit

002

The great outdoors, views, and fresh, clean air: spending time in remote locations surrounded by natural beauty is a healthy luxury for well-being and peace of mind.

003

When it comes to cabin design, windows are more than functional openings that satisfy light and ventilation requirements. They offer a design opportunity to frame views and enhance interaction between nature and architecture.

This small cabin was designed to provide a retreat for relaxation and quiet contemplation in harmony with its natural surroundings. It is located on a south-facing slope overlooking the town of Taihape with its layers of hills beyond, stretching to the Ruahine Ranges. Originally, the retreat was to be a studio for art practice and a base from which to explore the landscapes of the Manawatu-Rangitikei region. The brief then extended to require accommodation for occasional gatherings with friends. Locally sourced materials and technologies were implemented into the design of the cabin, limiting carbon footprint, optimizing energy performance, and building economically in this remote site.

AB Studio
678 sq ft

Copeland Associates Architects

Taihape, New Zealand

© Copeland Associates Architects

Causing minimal disturbance to the natural terrain, the cabin's structure consists of prefabricated panels assembled on a grid of supporting timber piles, raised well above the ground. The panels, manufactured from cross-laminated timber, form floors, walls, and roof all exposed and clear finished. Doors, kitchen cabinetry, and laundry benches are made from offcuts of the same material.

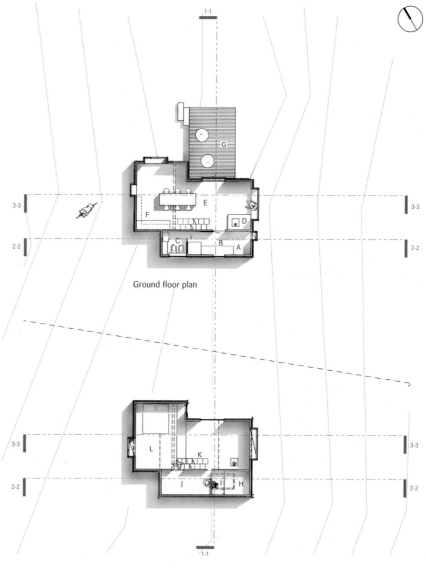

Ground floor plan

Mezzanine floor plan

A. Shower
B. Utility/laundry room
C. Bathroom
D. Hearth
E. Studio
F. Kitchen
G. Viewing platform
H. Platform
I. Turret
J. Loft
K. Mezzanine access
L. Bedroom

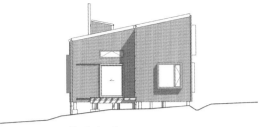

North elevation

Section 1-1

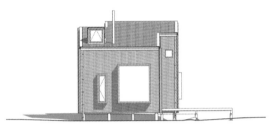

East elevation

Section 2-2

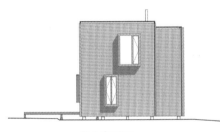

West elevation

Section 3-3

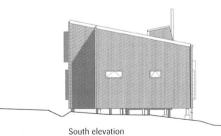

South elevation

The use of prefabricated cross-laminated timber panels was led by the desire for a solid, warm enclosure. Another advantage was the ability to build quickly. The precision-made panels were assembled on-site in two days. Followed immediately by fitting the aluminium windows, a weatherproof shell was ready for internal finishing and external cladding in just over a week.

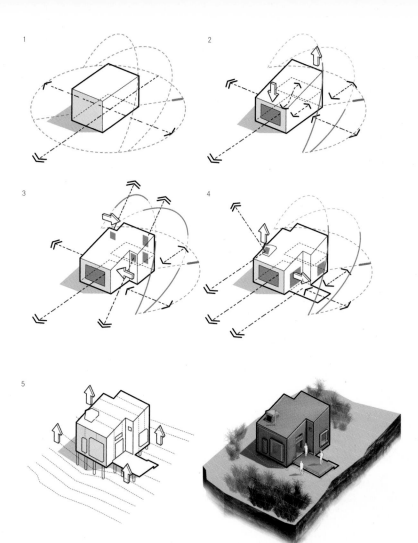

Environmental diagrams

1. Sun, site, and context orientation
2. Main view shaft, sleep, utility, and form modifications to inform internal layout
3. Pushing and pulling form to maximize daylight gain and opportunities for views
4. Pulling out the turret to the sky, activating the edges to the surroundings
5. Elevating from the ground plane to maximize views and pushing views out to activate wall edges

004

The use of locally sourced natural materials promotes the integration of architecture into its natural setting. Untreated wood, in particular, provides a rustic appeal, arousing feelings of warmth, coziness, and love for simple things.

Pallets, packing fillets, and CLT factory offcuts were all saved to make joinery fittings, including doors, cabinets, and benches. The high thermal mass of the CLT panels, coupled with good external insulation, provides a comfortable interior environment throughout the seasons. Wood, readily available locally, is used for heating.

005

The number and size of openings can influence the perception of spaces. Openings on various surfaces will make spaces look larger than they actually are, mainly because they allow in great amounts of light.

The Teitipac Cabin responds to the principles of sustainability, both in the use of materials—stone, wood, steel, and glass—and in the desire to create a cabin with a minimal environmental impact and harmoniously integrated into the hilly terrain of southwest Mexico. Built against a hillside, the cabin offers a series of spaces that immerse the occupants into light-filled spaces opened to the exterior and the expansive views, or into secluded and warm ones. The overall design is timeless, highlighting the beauty of its raw materials, which will weather over time, allowing the surrounding landscape to absorb the cabin, fusing nature and construction.

Teitipac Cabin
1,990 sq ft

LAMZ Arquitectura
San Sebastian Teitipac, Mexico
© Lorena Darquea

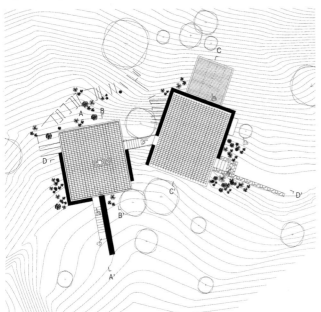

Roof terrace plan

Floor plan

Section AA'

Section BB'

Section CC'

Section DD'

Two structures, one containing the daytime spaces, the other accommodating the sleeping quarters, are connected by a glazed hallway, bringing natural light into the cabin's interior, while an external staircase leads to a roof terrace, optimizing on surrounding views.

006

The integration of buildings with
their natural surroundings is a
challenge that architects undertake
through a sensible use of forms
and materials.

007

To optimize the integration of architecture into its natural setting, the works must adapt to the physiognomic features of the site, taking into account morphology, climate, and cultural heritage of the region.

008

The adaptation can be understood as a long-term process in which the materials used weather with time, acquiring a patina that allows mimesis.

009

Architecture in natural surroundings reaches its strongest design appeal when it incorporates existing natural features such as outcroppings, trees, and vegetation.

010

Glass sliding doors, picture windows, decks, and roof terraces make for the ultimate outdoor experience in close connection with nature.

011

Modern cabin interiors are perfectly compatible with rustic cabin ambiance. The combination creates a cozy getaway atmosphere with a unique style adapted to a contemporary lifestyle.

Elsewhere, an Austin-area vacation rental company commissioned Sean O'Neill to design their first cabin. The goal was to create a compact living space with everything one would need for a weekend of focus and fresh air. The atmosphere that the architect aimed to re-create was that of a Texas porch, feeling the heat, the breeze, and the rain under the shade of a roof. A ten-foot folding glass wall allows the entire living space to become a porch. It was important that the cabins be functional off-grid. This would give guests a greater sense of detachment and allow periodic relocation. To this end, the architect designed the cabin on a trailer base with onboard utilities.

Elsewhere Cabin A

160 sq ft

Sean O'Neill

Georgetown, Texas, United States

© Sean O'Neill

012

Modern or traditional, cabins can be designed to be built in the workshop and transported to the site, cutting down building and transport costs, and saving time.

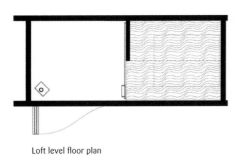

Loft level floor plan

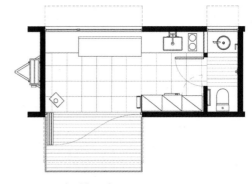

Main level floor plan

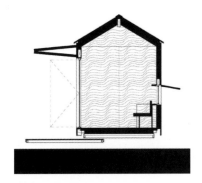

Section through living room

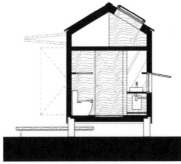

Section through bathroom

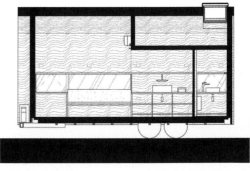

Longitudinal section

013

Contemporary cabin design
is taken to a new level with
transportability. Cabin owners can
take their home from one place
to another, exploring new natural
sites and escaping the everyday
routine of urban environments.

The architect avoided filling the miniature space with normal-sized house furnishings. Instead, he outfitted it with integral compact, multipurpose components. A single surface transitions from desk to sofa to kitchen counter.

The living space and kitchen counter surface continues into the bathroom. A frosted glass panel provides a faint view of the continued surface on the other side.

014

Minimalist fixtures and generous use of wood are reminiscent of Northern European architecture built for cold climates. Transportable cabins that are worthy of one's forest-dwelling daydreams.

Inspired by traditional shapes and the surrounding nature, Grand Pic Cottage is a unique architecture tailor-made for its residents. The owners wanted a warm space, fit to host family and friends. From the beginning, the design goals were guided by the site's topography and features. The result is a comprehensive reading of the magnificent woods in which it is located, offering a unique experience of symbiosis between nature and architecture. The clients' desire for a sober and warm retreat was made possible through a design steeped in simplicity, with each move guided by the aspiration to optimize the space's intrinsic qualities.

Grand Pic Cottage
1,460 sq ft

APPAREIL architecture
Austin, Quebec, Canada
© Félix Michaud

Site plan

The outfitting of a parking space allows
residents to leave the car and give space
to a pathway, from which the cottage
emerges through the trees. The pathway
transforms into a cedar sidewalk leading
to the cottage, composed of the main
pavilion and a shed.

Mezzanine floor plan

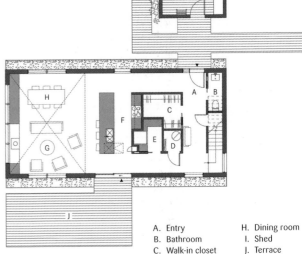

Ground floor plan

A. Entry
B. Bathroom
C. Walk-in closet
D. Mechanical room
E. Pantry
F. Kitchen
G. Living room

H. Dining room
I. Shed
J. Terrace
K. Bedroom
L. Master bedroom
M. Bathroom
N. Open to below

015

Traditional design and craftsmanship imbue rural modern constructions with old charm, taking cues from the iconic log cabin and the simple yet enthralling aesthetic.

In contrast to the black monochrome exterior, the interior overflows with light through its openings and the brightness of its materials. On the walls, the Russian plywood was highlighted. The wood's texture on all walls and ceilings allows the shape of the vernacular-inspired main volume to be accentuated.

016

Windows are one of the most expensive building elements, but they also allow for unique design opportunities, enhancing the spatial qualities of spaces, increasing a building's thermal performance, and adding to comfort.

The ground floor is organized around a central core partially integrating the kitchen. On the second floor, the core extends into a dormitory zone. Interior openings overlooking the ground floor spaces accentuate the influx of light and create a link between the two levels.

017

The use of simple, readily available materials can shorten building time, reduce energy, and minimize material waste. All this can result in cost-effective construction.

Stealth Cabin
1,500 sq ft

Superkül
Bracebridge, Ontario, Canada
© Shai Gil

This small family cottage was designed with a sustainability agenda at the forefront. Sited on a lake, it was important that the building integrates with its natural surroundings while minimizing environmental impact. The cottage is a sculptural form entirely clad in cedar, responding to the clients' desire for both a traditional log cabin and a modern weekend home. Dynamism of this material continuity is retained through the imaginative deployment of cedar in a variety of applications. Taking cues from its surroundings, the building takes its shape from an overturned boat found on the property, with the faceting of the cabin's walls echoing the rise and fall of the site's topography.

Cedar cladding traces the form of the
building from outside in, up the walls
and into the origami-like angular folds
of the roof, which rise and fall to create
dramatic, light-filled spaces.

018

Cedar shakes on the south facade
provide textural and tonal contrast
while thin horizontal cedar slats
form a screen that wraps the porch,
creating patterns of light and
shadow and modulating the view.

The cabin was sited to preserve a maximum number of trees, while its scale makes minimal physical and visual impact on the land. To reduce energy consumption, the cabin premeditates passive cooling and ventilation.

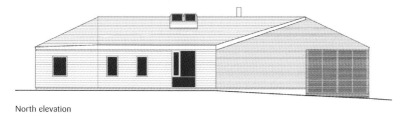

North elevation

East elevation

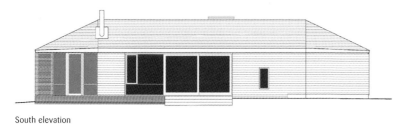

South elevation

West elevation

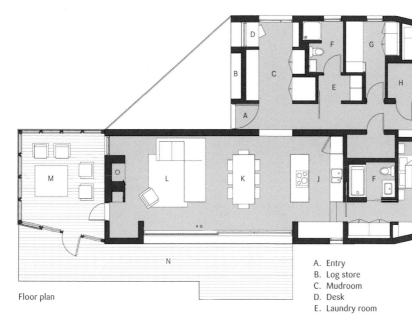

Floor plan

A. Entry
B. Log store
C. Mudroom
D. Desk
E. Laundry room
F. Washroom
G. Bedroom

H. Mechanical room
I. Master bedroom
J. Kitchen
K. Dining room
L. Living room
M. Screened-in porch
N. Deck

Large floor-to-ceiling wood-framed windows and doors overlook the lake to the south and provide ample access to a long cedar deck. As the untreated cedar boards and shakes weather and bleach to a faded gray over time, the cottage will appear to coalesce even further into its landscape.

019

The uniform use of one single material covering all surfaces highlights the spatial qualities of architecture, letting color, texture, and the effects of light enrich the space with visual nuances.

020

Materials with thermal mass are typically used in floors and walls where solar rays can reach them. The warm surfaces then act as radiators, distributing heat evenly throughout a space.

021

Built-in furniture optimizes the use of space, avoiding the need for freestanding furniture, which interferes with spatial clarity.

022

Built-ins also allow for a flexible
use of space, adapting it to
different needs and requirements.

La Pointe is a small shelter that is part of the Poisson Blanc Regional Park's accommodations. Surrounded by towering pines, it is ten minutes by foot on a trail from the visitors center. Its triangular geometry offers an interpretation of the legendary A-frame popularized in North America during the 1950s. It is a simple yet sculptural structure with steel roofing and cedar board-and-batten siding that provides functional and nature-oriented spaces. The shelter, which was built on-site by Atelier L'Abri's construction team, was designed to be off-the-grid, capable of hosting two to four guests. Leaning against the main volume, the covered terrace is the ideal place to enjoy the outdoors when the weather allows it.

La Pointe
400 sq ft

Atelier l'Abri

Poisson Blanc Regional Park, Quebec, Canada

© Ronny Lebrun and Jack Jérôme

Scale model

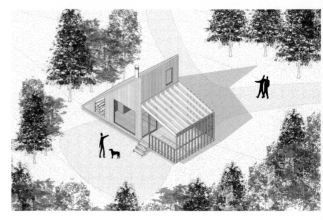

Axonometric view

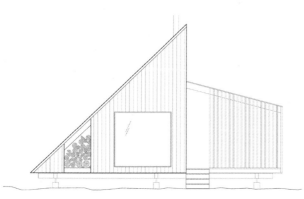

Elevation 1

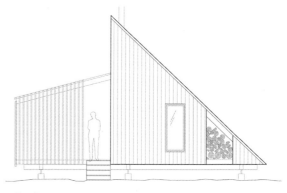

Elevation 2

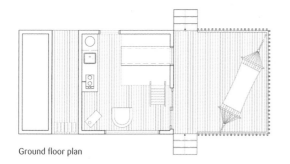

Ground floor plan

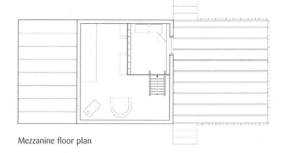

Mezzanine floor plan

The interior is minimal and bathed in natural light with a large window offering uninterrupted views of the forest. A kitchenette, a table that can be turned into an extra bed, and a sleeping loft provide necessary amenities for a short stay in the wilderness.

023

A retreat in the wilderness may suggest a rugged and adventurous way of living, but contemporary cabin architecture demonstrates that comfort is possible while out in nature.

024

The peculiarities of A-frame
construction conditions the use of
interior spaces, forcing creative
solutions to optimize the use
of space and take advantage of
awkward corners rather than leave
them as unusable spaces.

Tumble Creek Cabin

3,835 sq ft, including main
house, garage, and bunkhouse.

Coates Design Architects

Suncadia Resort, Cascade
Mountains, Washington,
United States

© Lara Swimmer

This vacation home is designed to be a net-zero carbon building—
highly energy-efficient and fully powered from on and off-site
renewable energy sources. Nestled in the beautiful Suncadia
Resort in Washington State, the cabin sensibly integrates into
its mountainside surroundings, blending sustainable modern
architecture with reclaimed rustic materials. The resort is
home to the beautiful and pristine Tumble Creek Community
that enjoys a 2,600-acre haven containing a rich and diverse
collection of amenities. Though the design team was challenged
by the extreme weather conditions, they were ultimately able
to create an elegant and comfortable space without the use of
traditional energy consumptive cooling and heating systems.

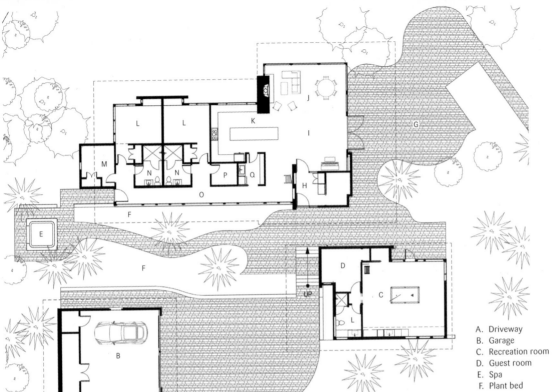

Floor plan

The architects sited the building to take advantage of passive solar strategies, including an ample sloped roof surface to support a 10 kWh PV solar panel array that provides all of the electricity required by the home.

A. Driveway
B. Garage
C. Recreation room
D. Guest room
E. Spa
F. Plant bed
G. Patio
H. Entry
I. Dining room
J. Living room
K. Kitchen
L. Bedroom
M. Bunk room
N. Bathroom
O. Gallery
P. Utility room
Q. Laundry room

0   8   16

Location map

North elevation

025

Roofs are prominent architectural features with a clear functional purpose. They unconditionally offer shelter, but roof design is, in great part, guided by climate. Some roofs can shed snow and rain better than others, some take the winds better, and others control the amount of light that enters a building through its openings.

East elevation

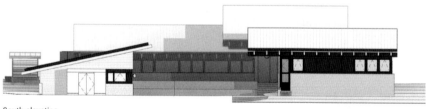

South elevation

West elevation

0   8   16

026

Exposed roof beams can add visual
appeal to cabin, craft-style, or
cottage construction, drawing on
the characteristics of wood framing.

027

Deep eaves respond to sustainable principles, shading walls in the summer and allowing sunlight in during the winter.

The dramatic cantilevered roof planes
utilize passive solar strategies by
shielding sunshine during the summer
and inviting it in the winter.

028

Clerestory windows, high ceilings, shed roofs, porches, and decks are typical design features in cabin and cottage construction that add character and relaxed appeal.

Vaulted ceilings in the main living and
dining areas are supported by exposed
steel and wood structural elements,
while floor-to-ceiling windows look out
on the landscape beyond.

A large board-formed concrete chimney commands attention as the focal point of the main living area. This solid mass, along with areas of concrete floor, also serves as a thermal heat sink to help maintain a stable and comfortable interior temperature.

The Driftwood Chalet is located on a gently sloping terrain surrounded by a natural landscape of impressive beauty. The development takes shape here, overlooking the Saint Lawrence River's estuary, humble and discreet like a piece of driftwood. The chalet is composed of two structures joined at right angles, creating a design that is as rustic as it is refined and offering a haven of relaxation. Its construction is reminiscent of the first homes with gabled roofs and rectangular masses built along the St. Lawrence Valley. The design addresses sustainability and cost-efficiency, enhancing a connection with nature to create a haven of relaxation.

The Driftwood Chalet
1,665 sq ft

Atelier BOOM-TOWN

Montreal, Quebec, Canada

© Maxime Brouillet

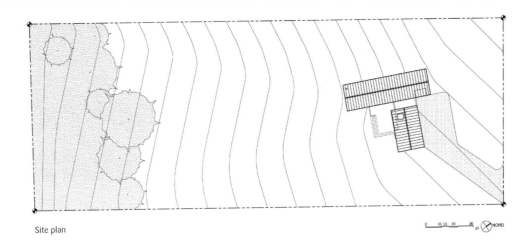

Site plan

West elevation

South elevation

Floor plan

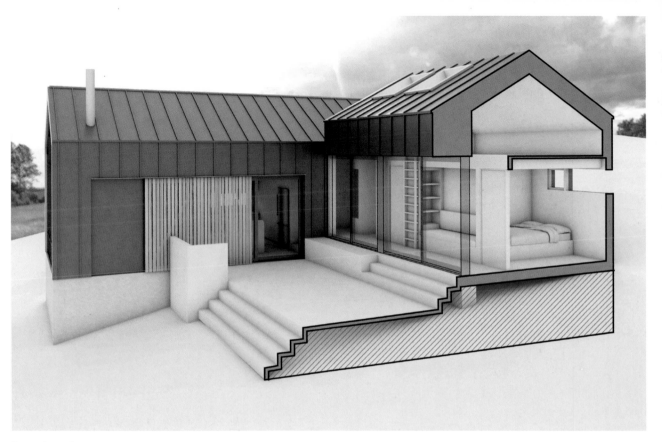

Perspective section

To ensure the construction was in harmony with its location, physical and virtual models of the terrain were created to design a project grounded on the land while maximizing the views.

The steel roof—which extends in places to protect the walls—together with the cedar cladding of the gables and parts of the sidewalls create a striking combination. The oxidation from contact with the sea air will gradually give the cedar the silvery patina that will further integrate the buildings into the landscape.

029

Gable roofs easily shed water and snow, while providing more ceiling height, and therefore an increased feeling of spaciousness. Also, in the interior, it offers opportunities for attic space.

A reading nook in the corridor leading
to the rooms faces a glass wall, offering
expansive views of the surrounding
nature. A ladder provides access to
a mezzanine—an extension of the
children's rooms below—offering a
space for play and relaxation away from
the world of adults.

030

A simple design and a limited selection of materials and colors emphasize light and views as prominent design features.

MARTaK is the first international certified passive house in Colorado. The project investigates how site-specific architectural design and environmental ambition can work in concert. The massing is inspired by the local mountains called hogbacks but also evokes a traditional cabin. The Passive House model shows the project —which is built off-grid—to perform at more than twice the certification level and experience has proven the standard to be comfortably reliable in reducing energy use to a bare minimum while improving occupant well-being and comfort. The project won the 2018 Green Home of the Year from *Green Builder* magazine.

MARTaK Passive House
1,275 sq ft

Hyperlocal Workshop

Masonville, Colorado,
United States

© Andrew Michler

Elevations

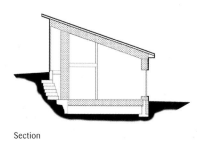

Section

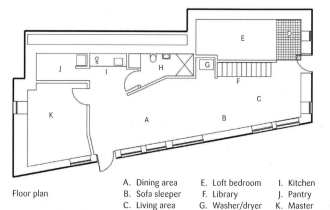

Floor plan

A. Dining area
B. Sofa sleeper
C. Living area
D. Net bed

E. Loft bedroom
F. Library
G. Washer/dryer
H. Bathroom

I. Kitchen
J. Pantry
K. Master
   bedroom

031

A simplified floor plan, a sunken shower, and an access ramp make the cabin accessible for guests with disabilities.

032

A building that can be reabsorbed
by nature after all non-natural
materials have been removed
for recycling is the ultimate
sustainable goal.

The design draws from contemporary small residential Japanese architecture utilizing an open floor plan and a restrained material palette. Along with the copious use of FSC plywood and lumber are a nail-lam wall and floor, ceramic and slate tile, and cedar pickets.

A step *tansu* staircase made from simple boxes anchors the elongated living space while providing useful storage. The small loft features a net bed, which gives kids a place to nest while providing daylight and an acoustic and visual connection with the main floor.

033

The home's angled south face and asymmetrical interiors reduce complexity responding to the Passive House Planning Package energy modeling, which encourages simpler shapes for efficiency.

034

Compact kitchen units come as
one unit or in a few pieces that
are meant to be assembled. They
make the most of limited space
providing full or partial service.
They are ideal for small temporary
accommodations such as mountain
refuges or beach cottages.

Wide window ledges provide small breakout spaces for a more intimate experience with nature outside.

035

Physical disability should not prevent someone from enjoying the log cabin experience. Extra-wide doorways, wide turning spaces, curbless showers, and countertop heights are adjusted to ADA requirements.

Located on a peninsula extending into Hood Canal, this house draws inspiration from the site and the client's Danish roots. Using the Danish sommerhus as a starting point, clean and simple forms clad in stained cedar sit quietly in the landscape, straddling the transition between forest and meadow. Public and private functions are divided into two gabled volumes, turned at an angle to provide a spacious entry and to access specific views. The site's original structure was moved, reoriented, and remodeled to serve as a bunkhouse, defining the entrance and enclosing the meadow's edge.

The Coyle
1,700 sq ft

Prentiss + Balance + Wickline Architects

Quilcene, Washington, United States

© Alexander Canaria, Taylor Proctor

036

Sustainable strategies are increasingly implemented in the development of land and construction, reducing negative environmental impact.

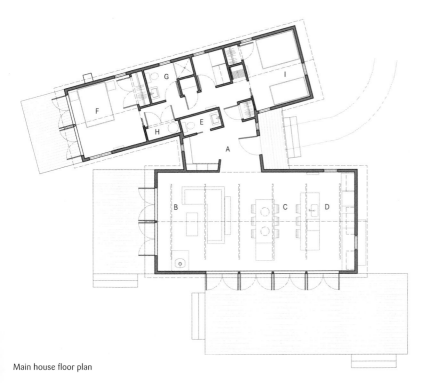

Site plan

A. Relocated bunkhouse
B. Existing bunkhouse
C. Main house

Main house floor plan

A. Entry
B. Living area
C. Dining area
D. Kitchen
E. Powder room
F. Master bedroom
G. Bathroom
H. Laundry/utility room
I. Bedroom

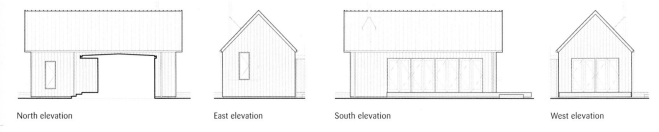

North elevation East elevation South elevation West elevation

Main house: main space

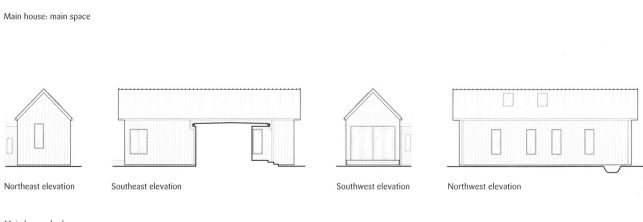

Northeast elevation Southeast elevation Southwest elevation Northwest elevation

Main house: bedrooms

The design has no grand style gestures.
Rather it focuses on functionality allowing
for comfortable accommodation while
allowing the surrounding natural setting
to take center stage.

A narrow floor plan and numerous operable windows allow for generous natural light and ventilation. French doors extend the living space onto adjacent decks and the meadow beyond, toward expansive views of Hood Canal.

The interior detailing of the house is clean and economical. White walls, pine floors, and wood trim create a light, warm tone within the airy spaces, while darker elements like the collar ties and countertops recall the dark-stained exterior.

The master bedroom at the edge of the meadow captures an intimate view of the Olympic Mountains and harbor, filtered by the firs.

037

Highlighting the architectural
character of cabins can be
achieved through detailing that
evokes nature, openness, and
historically motivated features
such as gable roofs.

The white surfaces enhance the spatial qualities of the cabin's interior, highlighting its form, scale, and materiality while infusing the atmosphere with serenity.

Contemporary retreats are designed to cater to a much more modern consumer, featuring sleek finishes, technological amenities, and abundant glazed surfaces to create an airy and relaxed atmosphere.

Window on the Lake
1,500 sq ft

yh2 architecture

Lac Plaisant, Quebec, Canada

© Francis Pelletier

This cottage is sited in a small green patch on a family property, just steps away from the Lac Plaisant's shores. Its simple, restrained, and refined aesthetic embodies the essence of cottage life, a wooden home designed for vacations and enabling true communion with nature. The home is a pure, light volume resting on its almost invisible foundation. Its scale is modest in its relationship with the surroundings, and its simple design exudes a relaxed character in line with the calm lake. Featuring a ballon framing and wood finishes inside and out, the house's single large gable covers all the living spaces as an expression of a gentle, simple lifestyle.

The south side is all glass, creating a
direct link between the lake and the
living spaces, arranged under a large
double-height gable extending outward
to cover a small porch.

The exterior, both roof and walls, is
clad entirely in white cedar boards.
Both of the building's long sides feature
three large, tall glass panels, allowing
seamless transitions between interior
and exterior spaces.

039

Technological advances in the
window manufacturing industry
allow for generous fenestration
with high thermal performance to
ensure interior comfort.

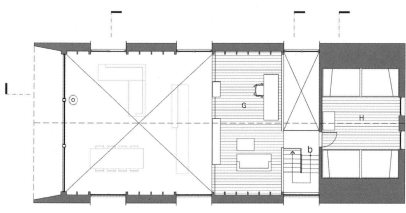

Upper floor plan

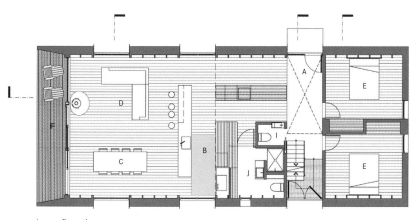

Lower floor plan

A. Entry
B. Kitchen
C. Dining room
D. Living room
E. Bedroom

F. Terrace
G. Office
H. Bunk beds room
I. Powder room
J. Bathroom

040

Balloon framing is formed by small wood members extending the full height of a building—generally two floors—from the foundation to the rafter, as opposed to platform framing, in which each floor is framed separately.

The balloon frame, with its exposed, painted white wooden studs and joists, gives the building a unique rhythm of shadow and light.

The full transparency of the southern facade lets in ample sunlight in fall and winter, while the mature trees standing between house and lake moderate the summer sun and provide a high degree of privacy in the boating season.

The interior is simple, airy, and light-filled. Floor-to-ceiling windows connect the interior with the exterior, providing the cabin with a feeling of amplitude and calm ensuring a relaxing stay surrounded by nature.

041

Exposed framing offers a rough look providing interior spaces with character. It also creates a multitude of design opportunities for storage.

The cottage, built in the 1960s on an enchanting site of the Laurentians, presents the characteristic form of an A-frame construction. Once the interior was demolished and the structure completely cleared from the inside, the architect exploited the triangular structural form. The monotony of a pre-established spatial organization was rejected in favor of a new layout that provides a relaxing feeling for this family retreat away from urban frenzy. These choices generated a rhythmic plan, resulting in a compact floor plan which gives the rehabilitation balance and coherence, offering much more in quality than it loses in quantity.

A-frame Renovation
690 sq ft

Jean Verville Architecte
Saint Adolfe D'Howard,
Quebec, Canada

© Maxime Brouillet

The design vocabulary of the
A-frame Renovation project follows
a minimalistic approach, highlighting
the emblematic A-frame form and
expressing the exterior skin of the
structure with a unifying color: black.

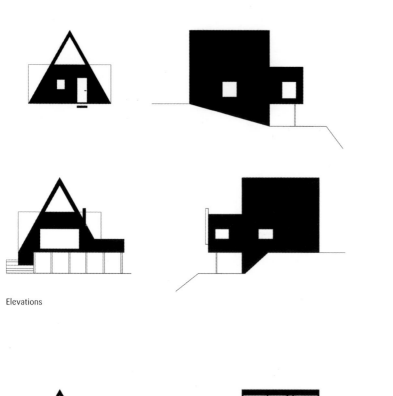

Elevations

Sections

Upper floor plan

Lower floor plan

The four elevations are pierced with
new openings pointing sometimes to
the lake, sometimes to the sky, to better
converse with the landscape.

The design reflects the architect's reflections on compact domestic spaces transgressing standardization. Challenging the initial hypothesis of lack of space, the architect opted instead for subtracting floor areas in favor of a rich spatial experience.

042

Prioritize the quality of space over square footage whenever possible, creating living spaces that are engaged with their surroundings, are adequately proportionate, and offer comfort and functionality. Larger spaces are not necessarily the answer.

The kids' playful den on the ground floor offers a storage platform under the beds and a reading corner nestled in a triangular alcove. This room, all in wood, reveals a fascinating place entirely dedicated to childish games away from the living spaces.

043

Increase the perception of space through openings on various surfaces, and through light colors, which will reflect the light.

Ingeniously playing with scales, Verville managed to increase the perception of visual depth by exploiting limits and openings to admirably draw part of the density of this space.

The project site has a working cattle farm, which the family purchased in 1981. It was originally part of a strip mine, and through their stewardship, has been reclaimed by forest, grasslands, and lakes. The Hut sits amongst trees, atop a high bank overlooking a lake. Its design was inspired by the Scandinavian concept of *hygge*, which can be described as a feeling of cozy contentment and well-being through the enjoyment of simple things in life. A build team comprised of family and friends constructed the cabin. Heavily influenced by aspects of farming, they used building techniques born out of tradition and logic, with simple materials used economically.

The Hut
600 sq ft

Midland Architecture

Belmont County, Ohio, United States

© Lexi Ribar

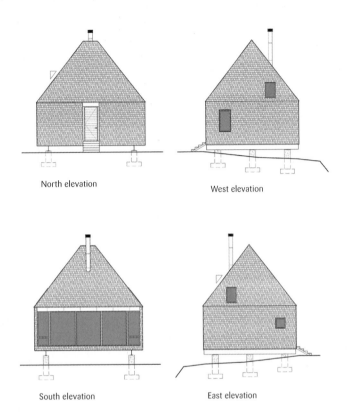

North elevation

West elevation

South elevation

East elevation

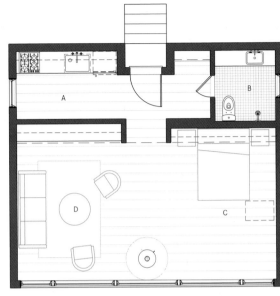

Floor plan

A. Kitchen
B. Bathroom
C. Bedroom
D. Living room

Responding to the principles of
sustainability, the cabin sits on a
simple foundation of concrete piers
to minimize its environmental impact.
It runs off solar power and collected
rainwater, satisfying the desire for an
off-grid retreat.

The cabin has a treehouse feel thanks to its location atop a high bank surrounded by trees. The cedar shingle-clad exterior melds the cabin into the surrounding forest minimizing its presence into the otherwise undisturbed landscape.

Designed for peace of mind, the outside
setting is brought in through a wide
expanse of floor-to-ceiling windows.
The simple interiors feature bleached
Eastern pine floors and white-painted
wall paneling. The pared-back aesthetic
allows the outside landscape to be ever
more present in the interior.

044

Bring in raw materials, neutral colors, and soft textures for a calm and comfortable atmosphere complete with the soothing effect of nature.

The overall design for the retreat demonstrates an emphasis on craft, in a style that the builders of The Hut like to call Country Minimalism.

045

Country and crafts styles—among others—are generally the most suitable styles for cottage and cabin interiors in keeping with an organic architecture that engages with a natural setting.

Skylights provide views of the tree canopy, bringing nature into the cabin and giving the impression of staying in a treehouse.

046

Contemporary and cozy can coexist. Combine clean lines with organic elements to achieve an atmosphere that is unpretentious yet elegant and attuned to nature.

Hyytinen Cabin replaces an existing structure, capitalizing on its spectacular location by a lake. The design consists of two stacked volumes over a basement. The first floor establishes a new relationship with the site. While the original structure was facing east, the new first floor faces south. This allows for a fully glazed narrow east end to open the great room up to the unobstructed views of the lake. A south-facing deck provides a sunny place to sit during mild weather. The second floor is oriented perpendicular to the first, cantilevering over the deck to provide a covered entry and shady place to spend hot summer days.

Hyytinen Cabin

2,144 sq ft

Salmela Architects

St. Louis County, Minnesota, United States

© Paul Crosby

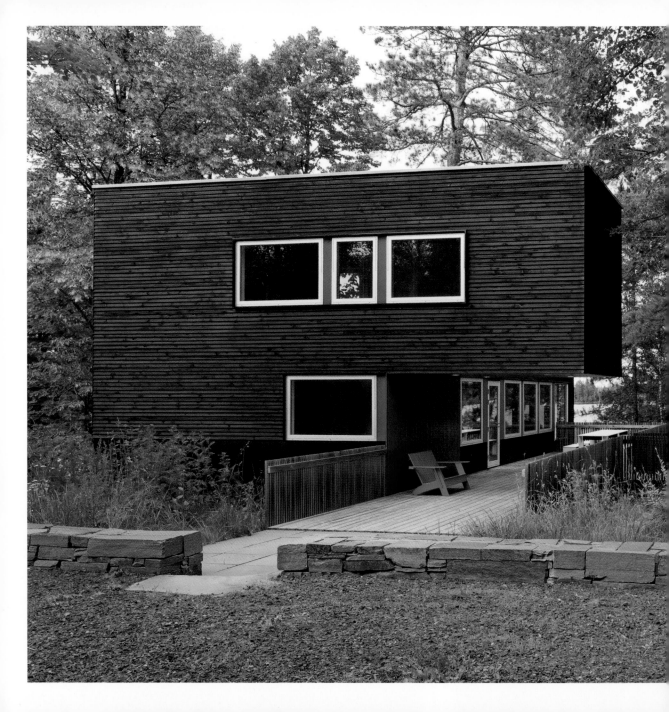

The exterior is clad in western red cedar stained with a traditional Scandinavian tar treatment. The natural texture of the cedar contrasts with the smooth matte finish of a black Richlite splash base. Deep blue accents complement the pinkish-red door of an existing cinder block sauna.

The fenestration and creation of outdoor spaces are perhaps the most effective design elements to engage a building with its natural surroundings.

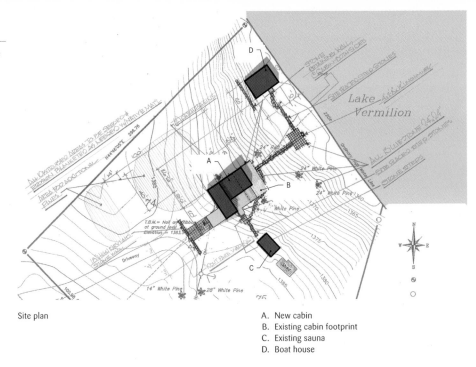

Site plan

A. New cabin
B. Existing cabin footprint
C. Existing sauna
D. Boat house

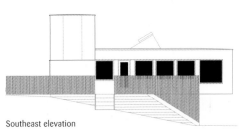

Southeast elevation

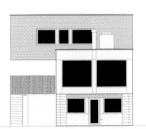

Northeast elevation

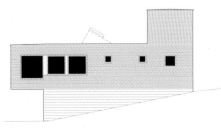

Northwest elevation

Southwest elevation

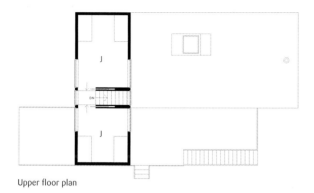

Upper floor plan

Physical and environmental conditions affecting a site guide the form, composition, and materiality of a building.

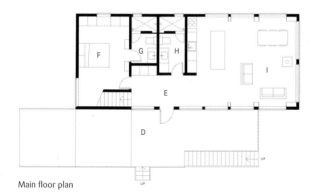

Main floor plan

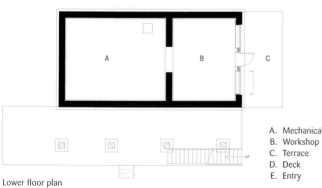

Lower floor plan

A. Mechanical room
B. Workshop
C. Terrace
D. Deck
E. Entry
F. Master bedroom
G. Master bathroom
H. Bathroom
I. Great room
J. Bedroom

049

Locally sourced stone used for dry-laid walls, steps, and pathways provide a wonderful character and contextual appropriateness in rugged settings.

050

Outdoor decks and terraces
are extensions of interior living
spaces capable of accommodating
activities that usually take place
indoors, such as lounging, eating,
and entertaining.

Interior walls are finished with local basswood. The pale color of the wood reflects the sunlight, adding comfortable warmth to the cabin's interior. Floor-to-ceiling windows and glass doors capture the views of the idyllic wooded site.

Week'nder

1,600 sq ft

Lazor / Office Design

Madeline Island, Wisconsin,
United States

© George Heinrich

Designed for a family of three and their guests, the Week'nder
is open and airy, taking in the beauty of the natural setting in all
directions. Due to the high cost of construction on the island,
the cabin was conceived as a prefab formed by two modules,
which were transported to the island by ferry. All of the cost-
intensive aspects of the construction, were integrated into
the prefab modules. A large room of panelized construction
and pitched roof was installed in the space between the two
modules. Natural and readily available materials—plywood,
pine, and corrugated and flat metal sheets—lend the cabin a
rustic feel balanced by color and texture contrasts. Inspiration
was the site itself, defining the experience at the Week'nder.

The Week'nder opens and closes, its
facades shifting from dark and opaque
to light and transparent. The two
parallel modules set a datum line above
which a gable roof rises like a tent.

051

Metal fins outside the windows of the two long sides of the cabin act as shading devices, minimizing heat gain and glare. Moreover, the window side of the fins is painted white to reflect the light toward the interior spaces. They are centered at the foot of the built-in-beds evocative of a ship berth.

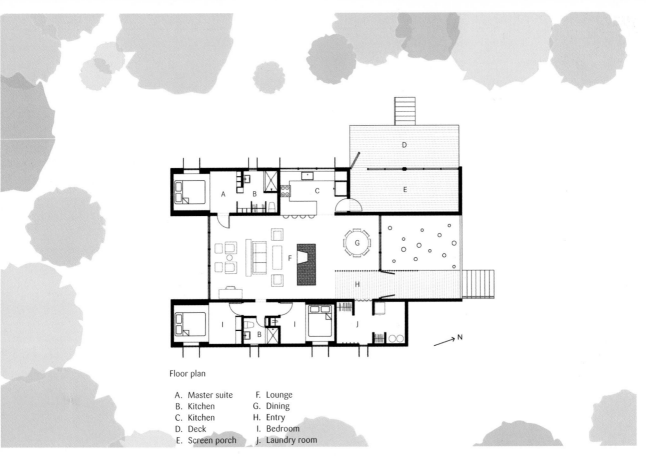

Floor plan

A. Master suite
B. Kitchen
C. Kitchen
D. Deck
E. Screen porch
F. Lounge
G. Dining
H. Entry
I. Bedroom
J. Laundry room

A screen porch extends the western module, offering a unique and sheltered semi-outdoor space facing the forest, while floor-to-ceiling windows on two sides of the central lounge open the cabin to the surroundings.

The duality created by opaque and transparent surfaces on the cabin's exterior is taken to the interior through screens made of thin posts, separating spaces, while maintaining an open plan feel and enhancing the shifting qualities of daylight. Interior and exterior is blurred by the prairie grass that rolls into a kind entry court.

052

The articulation of interior spaces through semitransparent partitions allow the separation of functions while maintaining a considerably open feel.

053

Clerestory windows are architectural features that add visual interest to a building while allowing generous natural light and glimpses of seasonal foliage and the different colors of light from dusk to dawn to illuminate the interior.

054

Prominent features such as the fireplace and kitchen peninsula create precincts of space for specific uses and guide spatial circulation avoiding walls and other types of partitions, creating a voluminous open space, atypical of prefabricated houses.

Folly Cabins is an off-grid small construction that addresses the importance of integrating architecture within its environment and the relevance of sustainable development. It brings a big experience and allows for disengagement from the norm and the expected while bringing an element of modern aesthetic and technological innovation. Folly allows for inclusive experiences such as work retreats, social groups, or intimate events. Utilizing architecture as a medium, these spaces will provide moments of disconnect in which guests can experience a creative escape.

Folly Cabins
1,000 sq ft

Cohesion
By Malek Alqadi

Joshua Tree, California,
United States

© Sam Frost Photography

055

In keeping with an off-grid style, home automation technology allows guests to monitor energy consumption and solar production, control secured entry, lighting, solar-powered skylights, and manage cooling and heating.

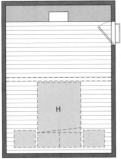

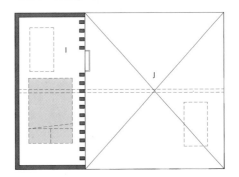

Upper floor plan

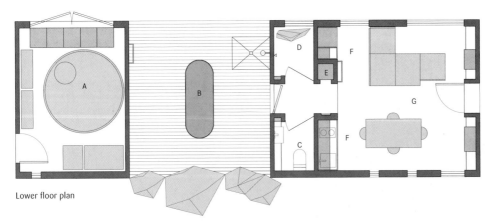

Lower floor plan

A. Equipment room and storage
B. Soaking tub
C. Water closet
D. Shower
E. Closet
F. Kitchen wall
G. Main space
H. Outdoor stargazing suite
I. Indoor suite
J. Open to below

A stargazing bedroom with no ceiling,
a shower with expansive views, and
an energy-producing solar tree is
the exploitation of nature through a
respectful approach.

Outdoor showers and hot tubs are not only about functionality but also about relaxation and pure enjoyment.

Attic spaces provide additional sleeping areas, secluded and cozy spaces, under the tent-like roof of a cabin.

The cabin's interior is compact yet space-efficient, using creative solutions to separate different areas and using windows to capitalize on light and views.

058

Secluded outdoor spaces extend
the season for outdoor enjoyment,
protected from the harsh sunlight,
heat and strong winds while
enjoying the views.

Country Home
3,030 sq ft

Julien Cardin

Lac Archambault, Quebec,
Canada

© Olivier Blouin

Country Home is on steep, wooded terrain bordering Lake
Archambault. Originally built by the current owner's father,
this family chalet required significant renovations to meet
contemporary living needs, including making it more comfortable
for the summer and winter seasons. The land features dense
vegetation, providing shade and cooling during the summertime.
The clients wanted to preserve its existing charm while creating a
modern, up-to-date environment. The addition of outdoor areas
for enjoying nature and the creation of spaces to facilitate year-
round sporting activities was a top priority.

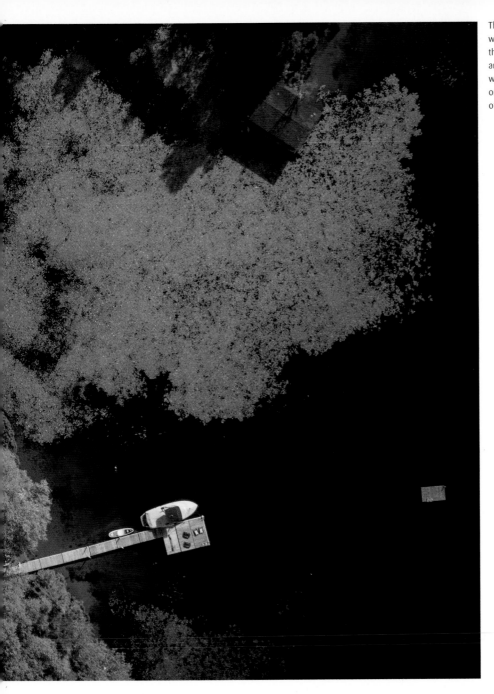

The existing patio, which faces the lake, was extended to connect with a new three-season space, creating an outdoor area for enjoying the sunshine. The solid wood railing was replaced by a glass one, giving way to an unobstructed view of the lake and lush vegetation.

059

In the design of cabins, the use of large windows and natural materials such as wood promotes the integration of interior spaces with the natural surroundings.

060

Use of a limited selection of
materials both on the exterior
and the interior contributes to an
architectural design that favors
simplicity and is in harmony with
the surrounding natural setting.

The original kitchen was reorganized and made to be open-concept. These changes made the space more functional, lending to gathering around a large island that has become a hearth of the home.

061

Wood and stone harmonize with industrial features to create a rustic aesthetic that resonates with a natural appeal.

With the renovation, Country Home meets the family's needs, no matter the season. It is now in perfect harmony with the original structure and nature, becoming a true haven of comfort and warmth.

062

Natural light enhances the beauty of wood, creating a warm and inviting atmosphere.

The Wooden Wing
3,500 sq ft

yh2 architecture

Lac-Supérieur, Quebec, Canada

© David Marien-Landry

The Wooden Wing is a large cottage perched on a granite outcrop, giving it a commanding yet intimate view of Lac Supérieur and Mont Tremblant in Quebec's Laurentians. The living spaces sit on a large, semi-polished concrete slab raised slightly above the natural outcrop, separated from the natural surroundings only by distinctive clear glass walls. A white cedar roof with ample eaves overhangs the glassed-in volume, protecting the living spaces from excessive direct sunlight and providing shelter for outdoor sitting areas. The house plays on the duality of openness and opacity, day spaces and night spaces.

063

Sensible siting is desired for minimal environmental impact, and protection against the elements while making the most of the site's qualities.

064

The generous use of glass
enhances the visual appeal of a
building's exterior, reflecting its
surroundings, merging architecture
and environmental context.

The use of a limited palette of materials—white cedar, polished concrete, black aluminum, and clear glass—both inside and out minimizes the boundaries between architecture and nature.

065

The site conditions will determine the type of glass to be used in windows and glazed walls, based on the thermal insulation and light transmission requirements.

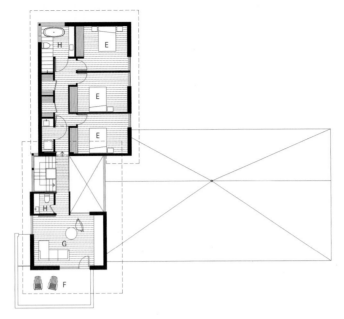

Second floor plan

A. Entry
B. Kitchen
C. Dining room
D. Living room
E. Bedroom
F. Terrace
G. Office
H. Bathroom
I. Garage

Ground floor plan

The roof above the open-plan kitchen, living, and dining areas tilts up toward the light and the views. It also extends well beyond the floor-to-ceiling windows to create a protected outdoor area.

066

Natural light can create uplifting
and energy-boosting places, while
enhancing the architectural design
of buildings.

The staircase is simple yet elegant. Its minimalistic steel structure, open risers, and wood treads harmonize with the two-story-high glass corner to create an airy and light-filled spot in the cabin that visually brings nature into the home.

067

Natural lighting is a way to keep humankind connected to the natural world, which is critical for a healthy lifestyle.

The site for this project is a remote, private lake beside which, for more than seventy years, existed a family's timber-frame cottage. When the land passed from mother to son, the decision was made to reinvigorate the home. Ultimately, because the home had already reached such an advanced state of decay, it was decided to have it removed and to build a new cottage. For sentimental reasons, the new home was to be the exact dimensions of the former, and it was to sit in the same location. Aside from the requirements, a far more open spatial arrangement was desired, but the character of the original wood home had to be reintroduced, albeit transformed with a modern architectural language.

Cross-laminated Timber Cottage
1,075 sq ft

Kariouk Associates

Ladysmith, Quebec, Canada

© Photolux Studio/
Christian Lalonde

Construction intentions were complicated
because the remote location meant that
skilled labor for stick framing would not
be available, and the cost of such labor
would be extreme.

068

The use of prefabricated parts needs to be decided early during the design phase. The goal is to minimize the cost of skilled workers on the construction site while ensuring the highest quality of construction.

Floor plan

Cross-laminated Timber Cottage **207**

The material selected was cross-laminated timber (CLT), cross-wise glued-laminated black spruce boards. These were brought to the site, where a helical-post foundation system was installed the week before, and hoisted into place. The entire shell of the cottage was assembled in less than two days.

While the technology to mill the
CLT panels is modern, the cottage is
identical in construction and materiality
to a traditional log home where fully
milled elements are simply joined
together.

069

There is no limit in the amount
and proportions of glazed surfaces
used in the design of a building,
provided that the glass offers a
good thermal performance to
respond to the climate.

Wood ornamentation was rejected
to emphasize the high-tech quality of
the CLT surfaces, which create a rich
and warm atmosphere. Exposing the
electrical conduits lends the interior of
the cabin an industrial aesthetic.

070

The way a building is oriented in relationship to the sun can have a considerable impact on heating and cooling.

071

It is important to orient a building to optimize sunlight when and where it is most beneficial while considering natural features such as trees or architectural elements such as roof eaves to control the amount of light. In the design of this cottage, the existing evergreen trees provide needed summer shade.

All the interior surfaces are clad in wood. With no ornamentation, the focus is on the visual and textural richness of the material. Only the windows framing the views disrupt such a homogeneous picture framing the views.

072

To highlight the richness of the wood, the surfaces are alternately left unfinished, or in the case of the bathroom, they are whitewashed. While the bathroom's floor is tiled, the rest of the cottage's is exposed CLT protected with a clear sealer.

Mini-Mod

684 sq ft

Framestudio

Sea Ranch, California,
United States

© Drew Kelly and Adam Rouse

This weekend home designed by Joseph Esherick and Associates in 1968 is one of a series of dwellings commissioned by the Sea Ranch developer Oceanic Properties with the intent to establish a community that appreciates and sustains natural beauty. The typical construction is an example of well-designed, ecologically sensitive, and affordable weekend homes. Because of their simple layout and small size, few of these homes remain in their original state. Framestudio sought an approach to the project that preserves the architectural intent of the structure while making functional additions that adapt the home to a contemporary lifestyle.

073

Spending time in nature reduces stress and increases pleasant feelings. Also, immersing oneself into the natural experience contributes to physical well-being.

The cabin's 20' by 20' footprint consists of a ground floor on two levels accommodating the living, dining, and kitchen areas and a second floor with two bedrooms. All the levels open onto one another, forming a loft-like space. The new elements were designed to respect the original architecture. In line with this criterion, a privacy door to the bunk room that becomes part of the panelling when open, keeping intact the open plan design.

Ground floor plan

Second floor plan

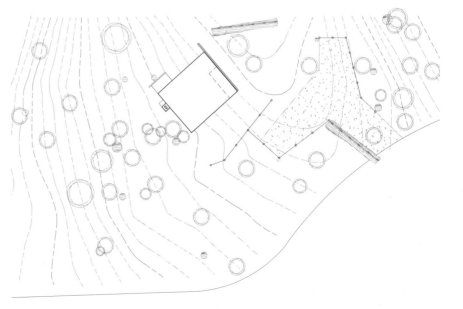

Site plan

The bulk of work on projects like these is, by design, invisible. This home received a down-to-the-studs update of the building systems and technology that brought the performance and comfort of the home up to today's expectations.

The Glass Cabin provides an off-grid family retreat with solar and battery power, designed and built by the architect. Reclaimed glass, restored prairie, and land entrusted to the grandkids were the genesis of the design. Nestled in a clearing of the woods near the Wapsipinicon River, the cabin provides great views of the native Midwestern prairie. Its environmentally friendly design began with a north-south orientation and a raised structure to minimize the disturbance of the grasslands and flood plain. The raised structure is essentially an agricultural modified pole barn/ wood frame structure. Natural materials were used throughout.

Glass Cabin
1,120 sq ft

AtelierRISTING
Northeast Iowa, United States
© Steven and Carol Risting

074

Well-designed sun control devices reduce heat gain and cooling requirements, while at the same time improving the natural lighting quality of interior spaces.

075

Operable windows and side patio doors provide additional daylighting and natural ventilation.

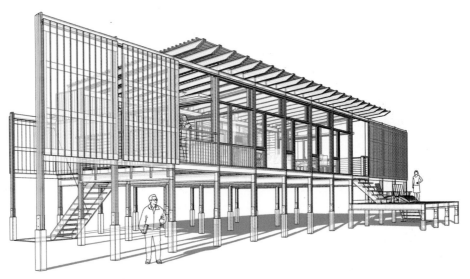

Perspective views

The extension of the front columns creates a manmade edge to the clearing in the woods next to the Wapsipinicon River. Barn doors slide open to reveal the northern glass front and close to provide security when not occupied.

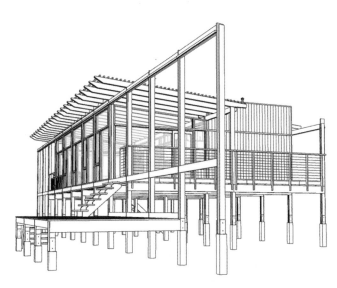

Large reclaimed pieces of clear and frosted insulated glass removed from a commercial office building expansion were used to create the north facade window wall. The reclaimed frosted glass was also used in the back bedrooms and toilet room to diffuse the southern daylighting and provide privacy.

076

A variety of shading methods can help, from fixed or adjustable shades to trees and vegetation, depending on the building's orientation, climate, and latitude.

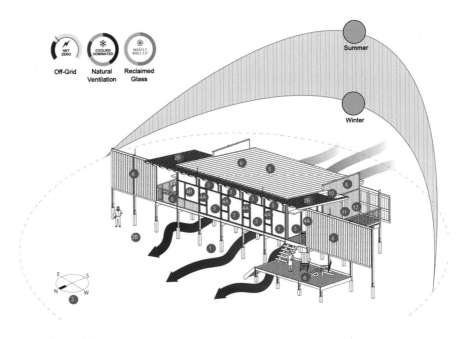

Diagram of sustainability strategy

The Glass Cabin is off-grid and thus net-zero with the following passive features:

1. Raised structure
   Allows flood water to flow freely below
   Minimum disturbance of the grasslands
2. North-South orientation
   2A | Northern window wall
   2B | Trellis for east and west shading
3. Reclaimed 1" low-E insulation glass
   Provides daylighting and views
   From a commercial office building expansion
4. Natural ventilation
   4A | Operable windows and patio doors
   4B | Screened-in porch
   4C | Ceiling fans
5. Wood-burning efficient stove
   Warmth and light

6. Western Red cedar structure, siding and decking
   Natural finish
   Water, fire, and insect-resistant
7. Minimum construction waste
   Standard lumber sizes
8. Insulated floor, roof, and walls
   R-30 floor, R-22 roof, and R-15 walls
   Mineral wool and rigid insulation
   + 2x6 wood floor and roof decking
9. White metal roof
   Minimize heat gain
10. Solar panels and battery power
    LED lighting
    DC motor ceiling fans
11. Compost toilet
12. Gray water filtration

North elevation

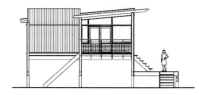

East elevation

Floor plan

0' 2' 4'   8'   16'

N

The 14' x 32' Great Room, with floor-to-ceiling glass on three sides, creates an experience of being outdoors, with northern daylighting and prairie views. A screened-in porch, east and west terraces, and a lower terrace complete the outdoor interaction.

077

The exposed rough-sawn structure, barn doors, exterior and interior siding, and exterior decking is predominately Western Red Cedar, selected for its natural moisture-resistant, insect-resistant, fire-retardant, acoustical properties and is a renewable resource.

The cedar surfaces were left natural to take a warm gray patina, referencing the aged barns in the area. All flooring is natural cork.

The kitchenette countertop is copper, and the wall cabinets are custom-built cedar with frosted glass doors. While primarily a three-season retreat, a Norwegian designed wood stove provides warmth for the holidays.

078

All-wood interiors are a throwback to simpler times. Inspired by traditional farmhouses, they celebrate comfort, cozy atmosphere, and life outdoors.

079

Barn doors are wide sliding doors that have made their way to homes, becoming popular interior design pieces that offer a rustic appeal.

The small cabin is sited on rugged and steep terrain with views over a spectacular fjord. Its compact footprint keeps to a minimum the environmental impact, yet the cabin offers maximum comfort, ensuring a pleasant nature experience. Taking the site itself as inspiration, the cabin's design stands out for its geometric clarity: A rectangular box topped by a triangular prism. The back wall facing the hillside and the side walls are made of concrete, offering protection against the harsh weather conditions of the region. In contrast, the front wall of the cabin is all glass, offering unobstructed views and taking in abundant natural light. The triangular prism is made of cross-laminated timber clad in black roofing felt, referencing vernacular buildings.

Cabin at Rones
506 sq ft

Sanden + Hodnekvam
Rones, Norway
© Sanden + Hodnekvam

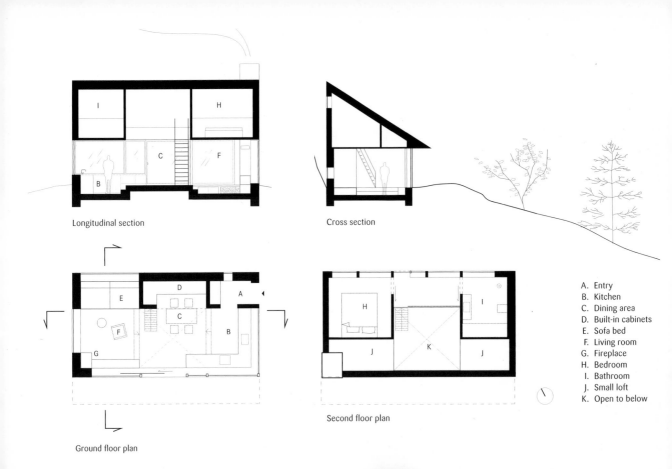

Longitudinal section

Cross section

Ground floor plan

Second floor plan

A. Entry
B. Kitchen
C. Dining area
D. Built-in cabinets
E. Sofa bed
F. Living room
G. Fireplace
H. Bedroom
I. Bathroom
J. Small loft
K. Open to below

The ground floor is organized on two levels adapting to the terrain. This allows for a clear delimitation of areas without the need for partitions, creating an open feel despite the small dimensions.

Site plan

080

Nature-inspired cottage and cabin designs can be taken a step further with natural features, such as outcroppings integrated into the design.

081

Multilevel spaces that adapt to
the topography, floors that extend
to the outdoors, floor-to-ceiling
windows, and materials that
mimic the colors of the natural
surroundings are design gestures
that enhance the architecture-
nature symbiosis.

A combination of concrete and Norwegian pine surfaces gives form to simple interiors, drawing attention to spatial quality, shelter, and the great outdoors.

082

The simple materials palette
creates a strong connection
with the land and roots the
building to its place.

The design of the cabinetry, made of birch plywood, is in keeping with the simple aesthetic of the cabin, which is equipped with no more than the most essential commodities.

Island Cottage

3,015 sq ft

Paul Cashin Architects

Sidlesham Quay, West Sussex,
United Kingdom

© Richard Chivers

Island Cottage was originally built in 1830, in a conservation area
on the South Coast of England overlooking Chichester Harbour.
The property was highlighted by the local authorities as a key
example of rural vernacular for homes in the area. However, the
original building had been extended over many years, mostly with
insensitive and cumbersome extensions and additions. The current
owners were greatly drawn to live on the South Coast after many
years working and living in London and showed a strong sense
of belonging to the area, as both had childhood memories of
visiting Pagham Harbour. After purchasing the property in 2015,
they decided to restore the cottage and reconcile its history of
unsuitable extensions to the surrounding landscape.

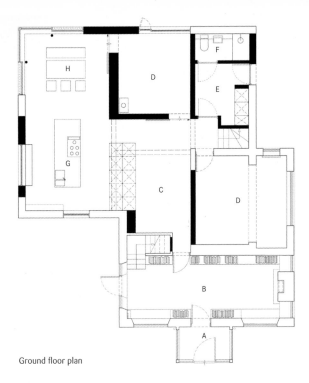

Ground floor plan

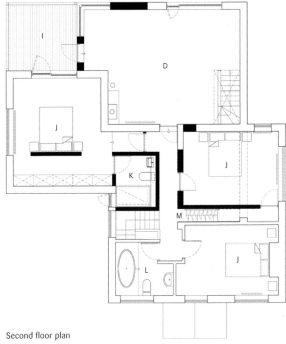

Second floor plan

A. Porch
B. Library/office
C. Hall
D. Reception room
E. Second entrance/
   utility room

F. Shower room
G. Kitchen
H. Dining area
I. Balcony

J. Bedroom
K. Ensuite
L. Bathroom
M. Roof access

To resolve the labyrinth of rooms
and corridors as a result of the many
alterations to the original building, a
single route through the house was drawn,
and a series of spaces were created to
reconnect it to the coastal landscape.

083

Architectural restoration's goal is to reveal and recover the original character of buildings to protect and highlight their heritage value, which is generally linked to the history and culture of a place.

084

Landscape design helps engage
architecture with its natural
surroundings through plantings
of local species. Hardscape and
structures are creative means to
promote a seamless transition
between architecture and nature.

The external facades were refinished with larch cladding, new timber windows, and a series of timber loggias set into the gardens. In the garden, native species were planted to take over the new timber structure to facilitate the integration of the house in its surroundings, which is vital given the local connection to the Sidlesham Nature Reserve.

085

The renovation of outdated spaces often involves the reconfiguration of the interior layout to improve circulation and adjacency between different rooms.

The ground floor plan was reconfigured
to allow a flowing movement between
the rooms. Views through and across the
house were opened up, restoring the lines
of the original cottage.

The client sourced much of the interior finishes and fixtures directly from salvage yards and online second-hand boutiques. The house is decorated with reclaimed materials referencing the worn and weary effect of time spent on the beach or at the seaside.

086

Renovation and upgrading should balance works to bring living spaces to contemporary standards while maintaining old-time charm.

The remodel of an existing mountain cabin highlights the spirit of the place at the edge of a densely forested area, taking into account the environmental factors that anchor the building to its natural context. ChAlet was originally built in the 70s and was being used for occasional stays. With time, it had fallen into disrepair. While the option of tearing it down and rebuilding it was first considered, the owners finally decided to restore it to its original charm. Changes focused on improving comfort and functionality, while the cabin's iconic A-frame was maintained. The sensible modifications contribute to the preservation of an architectural expression linked to the particularities of the site.

ChAlet

570 sq ft

Y100 ateliér

Donovaly, Slovakia

© Miro Pochyba and
Pavol Stofan

Elevation

087

Successful cabin designs celebrate
the spirit of the places where they
stand, incorporating elements
that are real, such as construction
materials, and conceptual, such as
the cultural heritage of the place,
through style.

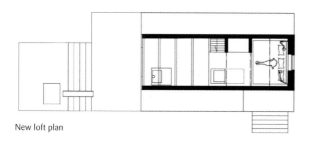

New loft plan

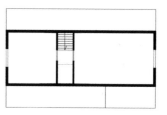

Original second floor plan

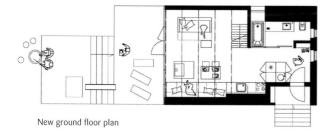

New ground floor plan

Original ground floor plan

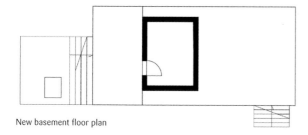

New basement floor plan

The ground floor plan was opened up to create a flexible space and to maximize daylight and views. The structure, roofing, and staircase were restored.

The most expressive element of the remodel is the glass front wall with an eye-catching glass door and bright green frame. In front of the cabin, a generous two-level deck with a playground, sandpit, slide, climbing wall, and sitting area connects the ChAlet with the surrounding forest.

Larch was used as the cladding material of the north wall and for the deck. Oriented strand board (OSB) paneling and oak kitchen cabinetry and flooring are the predominant materials used in the interior.

088

OSB is more efficient than plywood to produce. For its production, farmed trees are used instead of forest-grown. They are both, however, manufactured with PF resins, which emit low levels of formaldehyde.

089

OSB is an engineered wood panel similar to plywood when it comes to strength and performance qualities. OSB's combination of wood and adhesives creates a strong, dimensionally stable surface that resists deformation and deterioration mainly due to moisture.

The site is positioned on a plateau overlooking the fjord and two of Norway's most challenging climbing peaks. With dramatic far-reaching views, the cabin provides its occupants with a feeling of peaceful isolation and well-being, away from the hectic urban lifestyle. The layout opens and closes the cabin in different directions, turning its back to some neighboring retreats to the east, and opening toward a ridge and the close terrain on the opposite side. Its orientation takes full advantage of the sun exposure through the generous use of glazed surfaces balancing privacy and extensive views of the natural surroundings.

Efjord Retreat Cabin
2,150 sq ft

Stinessen Arkitektur

Eford, Lofoten archipelago, Norway

© Snore Stinessen and Steve King

090

Site analysis is a complex process that takes into account many contextual factors. The purpose of this analysis is to inform an architectural design in an environmentally responsible way, ultimately resolving the practical and aesthetic concerns.

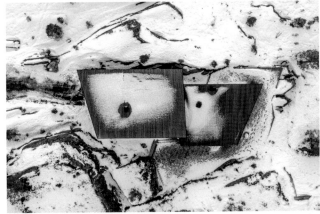

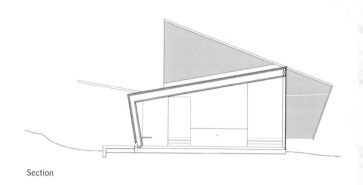

Section

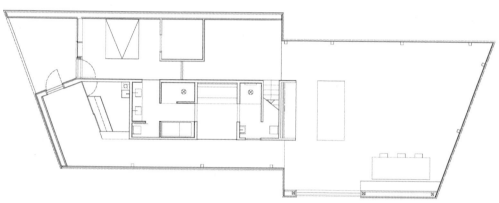

Floor plan

091

Passive solar and sustainable
construction expresses a more
opaque or a more transparent
building envelop to respond to
the environmental conditions,
such as orientation, climate, sun
exposure, and wind patterns
affecting every one of its sides.

The two volumes are offset to provide for sheltered outdoor areas, which merge seamlessly with the surrounding natural terrain. The orientation was carefully planned to take advantage of the views and optimize natural lighting.

092

An architectural design that balances light, views, privacy, and exposure to create a living environment that is sustainably engaged to the specifics of a site for maximum comfort and enjoyment.

The cabin design stands out for its form, clean lines, and minimal use of materials, including structural glazing and iron sulfate-treated pine on the exterior. The interiors are clad in birch. The granite floor, like the outcrops outside, extends throughout, blurring the boundary between the interior and the exterior.

093

Both pine and birch are typical of the region, widely used in construction for their strength and durability.

The sauna's bench, wall, and ceiling form a continuous undulating surface made of aspen slats. The wood contrasts with the stone, the other predominant material, creating a relaxing space in the cabin that harmonizes with the natural surroundings.

Culardoch Shieling

505 sq ft

Moxon Architects

Cairngorms, Scotland,
United Kingdom

© Ben Addy, Moxon Architects

Culardoch Shieling is located at the foot of Culardoch mountain—
"the big back place"—and looks out across the remote expanse
of upper Glen Gairn. It plays simultaneously off the informality
and romanticism of a Scottish hillwalkers' "howff," farmer's
hut or Swiss alpine shack, and the humanism and cleanliness
of twentieth-century modernists such as Aalto. Its exteriors
and interiors are clad in wood. The cruck-frame roof, covered
in moss and stone, has low-dipping eaves. Low and sturdy, the
construction blends with the undulating topography.

As if in a world unto its own, this small cabin sits alone in the vast, rugged, and windswept landscape of the Cairngorms, invisible from many directions thanks to the undulating topography.

The view through each window frames a specific aspect of the landscape: a bend in the River Gairn, the grassy flood plain, the water of Allt Bad a'Mhonaich tumbling down the side of Ben Avon, the massive granite tors on the summit plateau.

Conceptual sketch

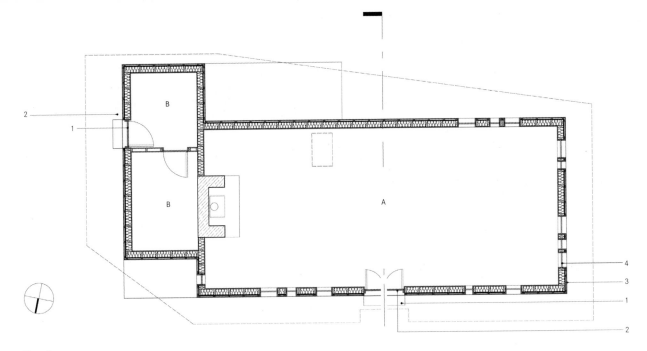

Floor plan

A. Great room
B. Storage

1. Larch step
2. Timber door with wavy edge larch planking
3. Wavy edged larch planking
4. Double glazed timber frame fix window U = 1.4W/m2K

094

Sod roofs are an efficient and sustainable approach to building in the environmental context, providing roofs and walls with a layer of insulation.

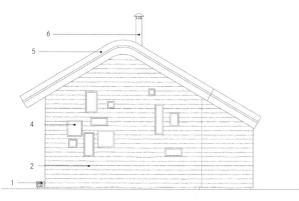

Southwest elevation

1. Larch step
2. Wavy edged larch planking
3. Timber door with wavy edged larch planking
4. Double glazed timber frame fix window
5. Barge board edge
6. Double walled, insulated, stainless steel chimney

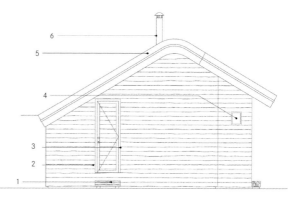

Northeast elevation

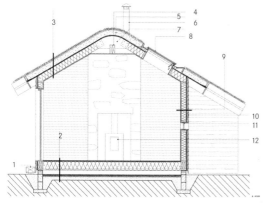

Section

1. Larch step
2. Floor assembly:
   - 15 mm engineered timber floor
   - 18 mm chipboard
   - 1 ply vapor control layer
   - 250 mm ISOVER space saver Ready-cut acoustic insulation between 50/200 mm joists
   - 50 mm solum
   - 1 ply 1200 gauge DPC forming seal against radon gas
   - 25 mm sand blinding
   - 100 mm compacted, graded inert hard core
3. Roof assembly:
   - 20 mm turf planting scheme
   - 100 mm turf growing medium in hessian sacks
   - 1 ply PROTAN Progreen membrane
   - 1 ply PROTAN 2B fleece
   - 18 mm plywood
   - 200 mm KINGSPAN KOOL THERM K7 pitched roof board rigid PIR foam (2 x 100 mm) insulation between 50/200 mm rafters
   - 1 ply ACTIS TRISO SUPER 10 + thin multifoil insulation
   - 20 mm horizontal Sitka spruce board cladding

4. 2 x 75/250 ridge beam coach boiled together
5. Turf roof
6. Double walled, insulated stainless steel chimney
7. Plywood gussets coach bolted to rafters
8. THE ROOFLIGHT COMPANY NEO top hung skylight fitted to manufacturer's instructions
9. Wall assembly:
   - 12 mm wavy edged larch planking
   - 25 mm vertical battens to leave air gap
   - 1 ply breather membrane
   - 18 mm plywood
   - 150 mm KINGSPAN KOOL THERM K12 framing board rigid PIR foam insulation between 50/150 mm studs
   - 1 ply Tyvek vapor control layer
   - 20 mm horizontal Sitka spruce board cladding
10. Wavy edged larch planking
11. Double glazed timber frame fix window
12. WESTFIRE 23 HETAS approved wood burning stove unit

095

Windows of various sizes
and proportions control the
amount of light and views while
maintaining an enveloping sense
of seclusion and security.

Makatita Tiny House is the result of a collaboration between a single woman who dreamed about a house in a forest and the Liberté Tiny Houses team, whose design philosophy focuses on the creation of living environments guided by sustainable development and environmental responsibility. The creative process embraces the art of slow living in perfect harmony with nature. Inspired by the forms of leaves, the design gives the cabin its distinctive geometric form of folded planes, offering different appearances when viewed from different angles. Built entirely with hand tools in the workshop, the cabin was transported to the site once finished.

Makatita Tiny House
215 sq ft

Liberté Tiny Houses
Location not specified

© Gijs Coumou /
Liberté Tiny Houses

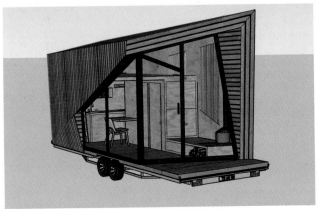
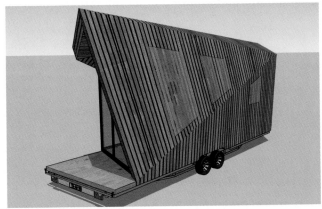
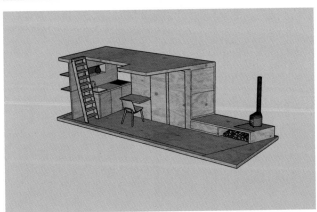
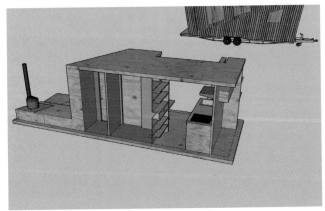

3D views of the cabin

096

Site impact should be controlled
by sustainable development and
environmental responsibility while
ensuring longtime sustainability.

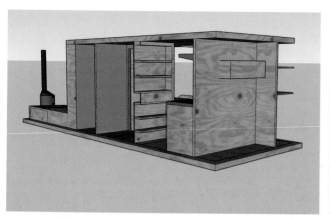
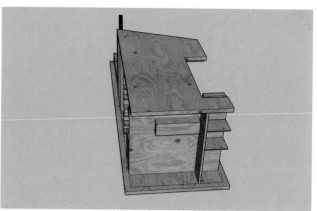
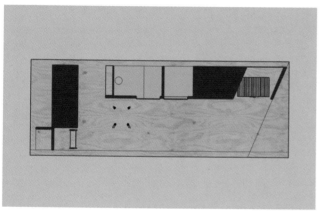
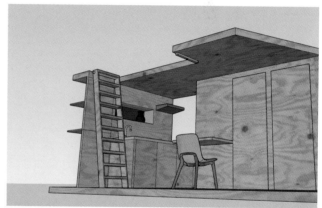

097

Makatita Tiny House is a good exemplification of slow living, which is expressed through the minimization of everything deemed unnecessary and wasteful. The goal is to reach a zero carbon footprint and a life in harmony with nature.

Nature-inspired architecture blends with nature rather than competes with it. This design approach was passionately defended by architects such as Louis Sullivan and Frank Lloyd Wright during the first half of the twentieth century.

Foor-to-ceiling windows minimize the separation between interior and exterior, optimizing the outdoor experience and connection with the natural surroundings.

098

Prefabricated dwellings start as parts that are manufactured in a workshop. Once built, the parts are then transported to the chosen site where they will be assembled.

099

Prefabrication offers a wide range of benefits: Its modularity allows for a flexible layout that adapts to different needs. Also, its affordable cost appeals to a wider audience, and its efficient use of materials reduces waste, responding to environmental concerns.

The cabin has built-ins to make the most of the compact space, maximizing storage potential, creating smooth transitions between areas, and promoting a coherent overall design.

Built as a nature retreat for meditation and creation, this mobile cabin stands at the edge of a forested area, facing an open field. It offers guests peace and quiet away from the noise of the urban environment. The retreat is nothing like the usual mountain or beach cabin. Its construction is minimal and devoid of any ornamentation. In the interior, furnishing is sparse to go with the raw and bare aesthetic. The atmosphere is monastic. In keeping with the religious appeal of the retreat, a series of interlocking wood panels cut to look like archways create a dome above the space, a place for guests to immerse themselves into their meditative needs or creative pursuits.

Forest Cabin Retreat
160 sq ft

The Way We Build

Robbenoordbos,
The Netherlands

© Jordi Huisman

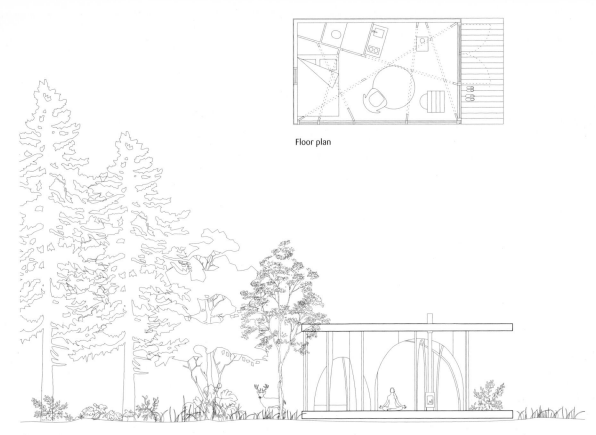

Floor plan

Elevation

Two of the four cabin's walls are shingle
clad, while the other two are fully
glazed, creating a sense of protection
yet opening the interior to the exterior
to experience the intimacy of the forest
and the expansiveness of the open field.

100

The environment of a chosen site sets the tone for the form and materiality of a building, creating a harmonious connection with the existing natural features.

101

Open plan setups and big windows
can make the outdoors feel as if
it's an extension of the interior
and encourage time spent outside.
Scientific studies show that spending
time outdoors strengthens the ability
to concentrate.

The interior includes a bed, a compact
kitchen, a wood burning stove, and a
compost toilet. A shower is in the shared
bathhouse onsite. All is conceived to
focus on the connection with nature and
the enjoyment of peace and quiet.

102

Minimal partitions make the most of limited space, while maximizing daylight and views, and promoting a sense of spaciousness.

The initial project consisted of a small bedroom hut with a bathtub. Gradually, as the conversations with the client developed, a new hut appeared to accommodate daytime activities. Eventually, a third hut was added to serve as a garage and utility room. The design of the cabins takes a cue from the traditional fishermen's huts in the area. These huts have a long history. With a design approach mixing sustainability strategies and attention to the particularities of the site, the cabins are functional and quick to build. They stand among pine trees, protected from the region's intense summer heat, and providing an atmosphere inviting to relaxation.

Cabins in Comporta
1,560 sq ft

Studio 3A

Comporta, Portugal

© Nelson Garrido

The charred Douglas fir exterior finish of the cabins offers a distinct, rich look, achieved through an ancient Japanese technique called Shou-Sugi-Ban. The resulting finish is known to be resistant to fire, pests, and decay.

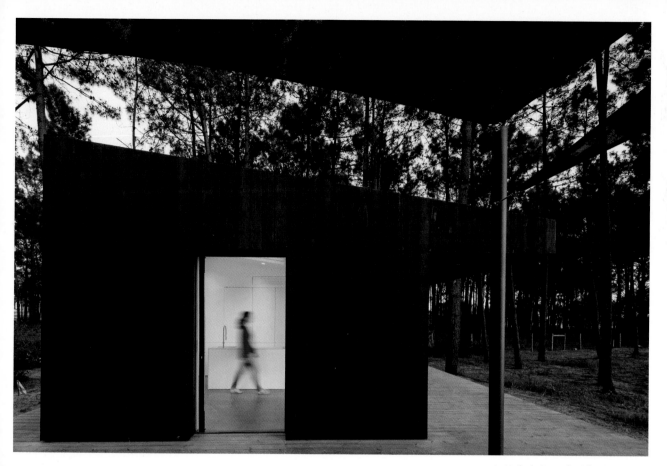

A simple design and quick construction make the Comporta Cabins an environmentally friendly construction that adapts to any setting with a minimum carbon footprint.

Key design features include overhangs above the windows, low emissivity glass protected from low hot sun by external blinds, and a tensioned fabric membrane, which creates a shaded area between the daytime and nighttime cabins. Sun exposure and wind patterns were key environmental factors that determined the placement of the cabins.

Studio 3A collaborated with MIMA Housing, another architecture firm with experience designing prefabricated modular housing. This is reflected in the use of OSB sandwich panels and joint systems, which contributed to the fast construction of the cabins.

103

Concrete floors offer exceptional thermal mass. They maximize heat absorption when stained dark. The stored heat is slowly released into the space as part of a nightime passive heating strategy aimed at eliminating the need for electricity for climate control.

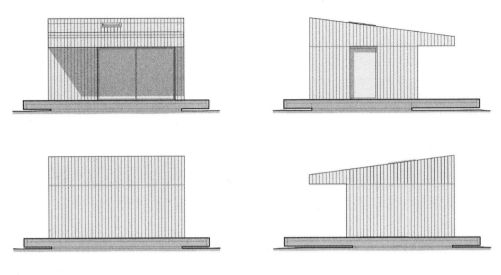

Elevations

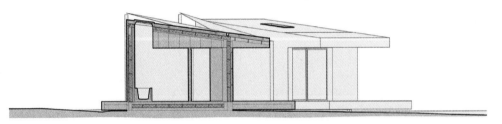

Perspective section

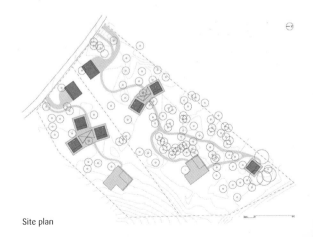

Site plan

104

Modular cabins are setting the trend for escape retreats, vacation homes, and secondary dwellings. They offer a unique look while providing opportunities for design flexibility and customization.

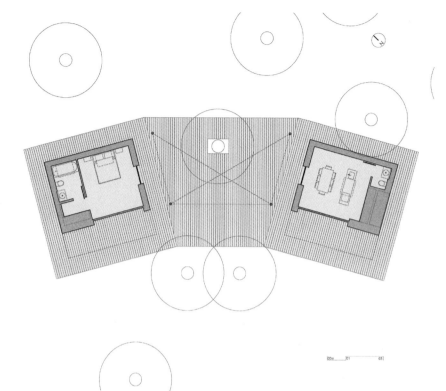

General floor plan

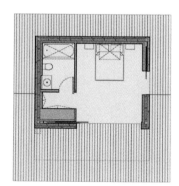

Module's floor plan

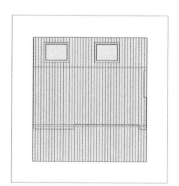

Module's roof plan

Building at high altitude has pros and cons. The Hooded Cabin enjoys magnificent views, but its design and construction were guided by strict building regulations. Cabins in the area are required to have sectioned windows, standing wood paneling, 22- to 27-degree gable roofs, and triple bargeboards. But perhaps there is nothing greater than challenges to break the mold. During the design process, these challenges were turned into fuel for creative thinking, resulting in a peaceful retreat of undeniable functionality and unique aesthetics. The cabin stands out from all other constructions in the area despite the limitations, offering a striking interpretation of the typical pitched-roof cabin.

Hooded Cabin
785 sq ft

Arkitektværelset
Imingfjell, Telemark, Norway
© Marte Garmann

The ore-pine roof tilts back to open
up the front of the cabin to the views
and the light while creating a protected
area in front of the entry.

105

Coastal development is regulated to protect, manage, and restore healthy natural environments for everyone's enjoyment.

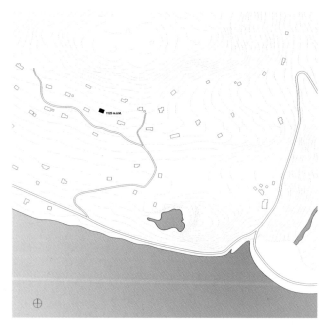

Location map

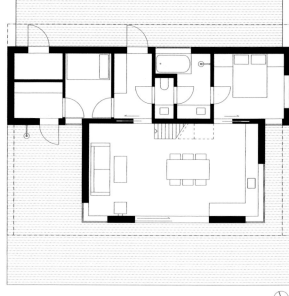

Floor plan

106

Good environmental stewardship
contributes to the creation of
unique architectural developments
while protecting sensitive areas.

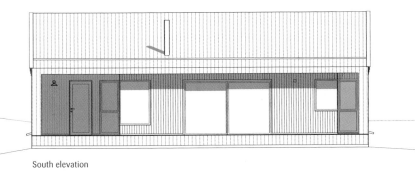

The clear-sealed ore-pine roof, sidewalls, and deck combine with the black-painted front and back walls of the cabin, creating an elegant contrast. Moreover, the slanted paneling of the side walls adds to the modern appeal of the cabin's design.

South elevation

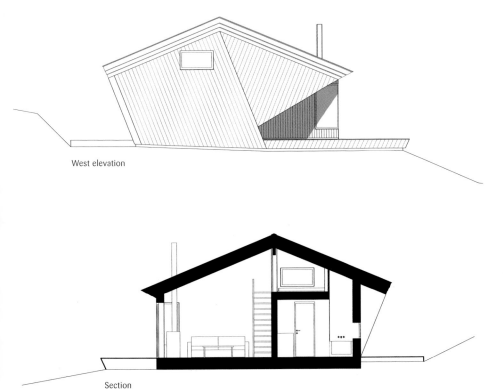

West elevation

Section

The panoramic windows and large sliding doors at the front bring nature into the kitchen living room. The interior features oak flooring and paneling, reflecting the natural colors of the surroundings.

107

Other than for minimizing visual impact, the integration of a building into the landscape is about making the surrounding natural beauty part of the building's character.

108

The use of natural materials such as wood and stone generates a look and feel that is reminiscent of the real log cabin.

Dômes Charlevoix
540 sq ft

Bourgeois / Lechasseur architects

Petite-Rivière-St-François,
Quebec, Canada

© Maxime Valsan

Dômes Charlevoix is a new concept of year-round eco-luxury accommodations in the heart of nature. The project consists of three geodesic domes that are the starting point of a larger lodging development with an environmentally friendly approach to tourism. Design decisions were aimed at keeping the carbon footprint of the development to a minimum. The domes, which can be accessed through a trail from a parking lot, are sensibly integrated into the natural surroundings. They sit on wooden decks and are carefully positioned, allowing guests to immerse themselves in the beauty of the natural environment.

109

Managing and reducing the carbon footprint is becoming increasingly critical. Buiding in an environmentally friendly way can start by using sustainable materials, and reduce energy waste.

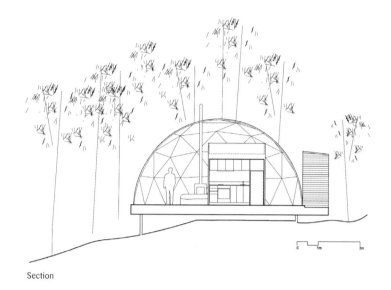

Section

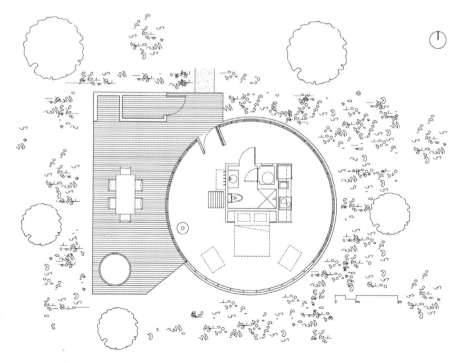

Floor plan

The structures of the domes are covered by a warm gray canvas made of PVC and insulation, making accommodation possible even in the region's cold winters. The domes, which can accommodate up to four guests, and are fully fitted for maximum comfort.

110

The use of materials, energy, or practices that respond to the principles of sustainability is aimed at limiting the negative impact on natural resources. For instance, carefully managed tree cutting allows forest regeneration at a rate that it can keep up with the need for wood materials.

Concrete floor radiant heat brings warmth, while the gray canvas and the stove create a cozy atmosphere.

A central service unit contains a kitchen, a Murphy bed, and a bathroom with shower. A ladder leads to a loft bed on top of the service unit.

111

Good insulation is crucial to ensure maximum comfort and energy efficiency. Strong, waterproof, and durable insulating materials should be used to create air-tight interior spaces protected against extreme temperatures, moisture, and wind.

A section of the canvas can be pulled back, opening the domes to the views and to natural light.

Mountaineer's Refuge

646 sq ft

Gonzalo Iturriaga Arquitectos

Comune of San Esteban,
5th Region, Chile

© Federico Cairoli

The design brief was for a small cabin that would serve as a base camp for an avid mountaineer. The building's low slung and irregular geometry echoes the morphology of the region's high mountains through folding planes revealing openings for access, views, and natural light. The cabin rests on piles, lifted off the ground, and rising to form a tentlike dark wooden structure. This is the point of arrival and departure for the mountaineer's adventures, a lookout, a shelter, a refuge for contemplation and rest between climbs.

112

Form and scale are architectural
elements that guide the design of
buildings to achieve aesthetically
pleasing and functional compositions
while promoting a sound connection
between the built form and its
immediate surroundings.

The exterior is finished in blackened
pine. Inside, the same material is
expressed untreated, a pale blond tone
contrasting with the black window and
door frames.

113

Consider the contextual qualities of a site during the initial design phase. New construction should reinforce the character of a specific place and set high standards in terms of its siting and design.

The spatial experience is guided by the volumetric qualities of the cabin. In that respect, its interior is a reflection of the exterior with only a central utility core, including a kitchen and a bathroom, to separate the different areas.

Site plan

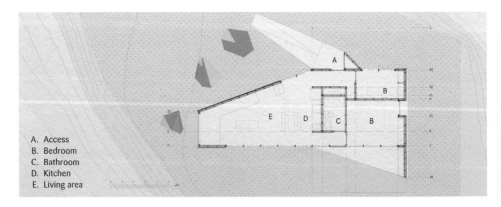

A. Access
B. Bedroom
C. Bathroom
D. Kitchen
E. Living area

Floor plan

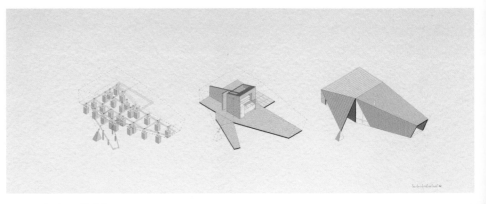

Axonometric views of building components

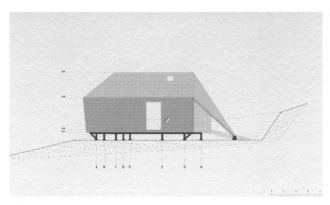

North Elevation

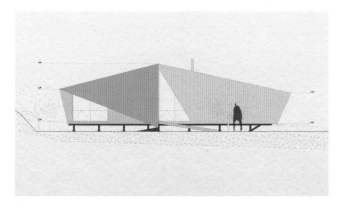

East elevation

West elevation

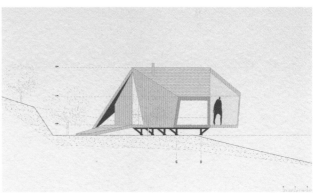

South elevation

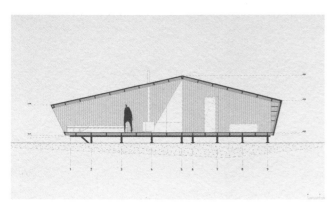

Section A

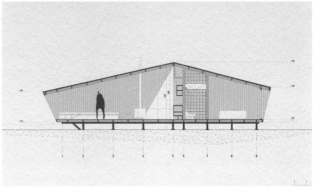

Section B

Mountaineer's Refuge **351**

114

Floor-to-ceiling windows encourage
an interior space to extend to the
exterior. This minimizes interior and
exterior boundaries and fosters the
integration of the built form into
the surrounding landscape, making
the natural environment part of the
architecture and vice-versa.

A series of dedicated openings provide cross ventilation, taking advantage of the updraft rising from the valley.

The Cabin Østfold is located in the Oslofjord archipelago, with great views to the sea, and the adjacent coastal landscape. The cabin consists of two structures—a main building and an annex—connected by a central terrace. The foundation of a previous building on the site and its architectural character established the limits of the new construction and informed the new design. This is reflected in the design of the roof, which takes cues from the traditional gable roof structures. While Cabin Østfold may incorporate elements of the area's vernacular architecture, it exudes a modern appeal that comes with the creative use of natural materials.

Cabin Østfold
645 sq ft

Lund+Slaatto Architects
Østfold, Norway
© Marte Garmann

The cabin's exterior and the terrace are built with cedar timber. The roof eave extends over the windows, limiting heat gain and glare but allowing the interior to take in the views of the sea.

115

The brise soleil is a popular and effective solar shading technique widely used before air-conditioning to control the amount of direct sunlight that enters a building.

The cedar terrace and roof form a continuous surface that protects the hillside of the cabin in a sheltering way while extending beyond and above the windows at the front of the cabin to allow for light and views.

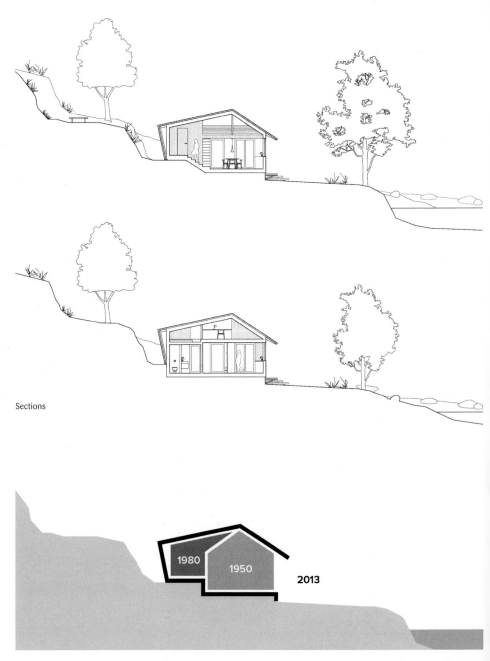

Sections

Diagram

1980

1950

2013

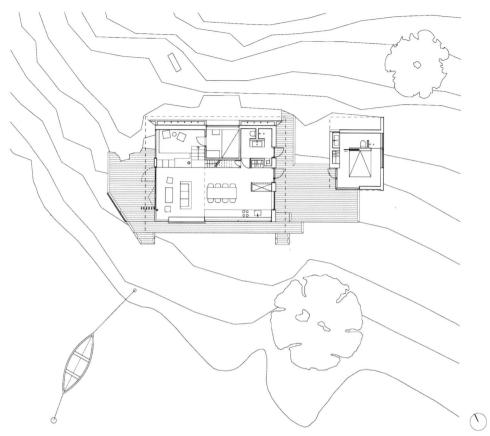

Floor plan

116

Geographical location, environmental and cultural context, climate, and orientation are factors that need to be taken into account during the design process of a building. These are some of the guidelines devised to optimize a building's adaptation to a specific site and optimize its efficiency and performance.

117

Avoid tall furniture to enhance the
sense of amplitude in small spaces.
With few or no cumbersome
pieces of furniture, a room can
also look brighter because light
can reach further in, and no
unsightly shadows are cast.

118

Protecting windows from sunlight is critical for good window management. How the sun moves through the sky should determine a building's orientation and the placement of windows to minimize direct solar admission.

The cabin's interior is an open
plan layout organized on various
levels, adapting to the site's sloping
topography. With minimal partitions,
every corner of the cabin enjoys the
views and the light through the glazed
sea-facing wall.

Sited on a clearing on a steeply sloping and heavily forested site, Woodshed is both a guest cottage and entertainment space for the main residence on the same property. The construction is conceptually inspired by the vernacular woodshed, a familiar and iconic element in the Vermont landscape. It is composed of two asymmetric gable roof forms, akin to the traditional woodshed. The two are connected by a central entryway. The design purposefully projects a minimal, familiar elevation to the non view, public street side, and an engaging, contemporary, open elevation to the private hillside.

Woodshed
3,500 sq ft

Birdseye Design

Pomfret, Vermont,
United States

© Jim Westphalen

119

The use of recycled materials
responds to principles of
sustainability while providing a
building with a rustic appeal. This
could especially apply to rural
construction, where the goal is
to integrate architecture into its
natural surroundings and evoke
elements of vernacular heritage.

The siding is composed of repurposed corral fencing boards. Great effort was made to minimize the amount of detailing and simply express the natural beauty of the weathered material.

The scrim wall is composed of several board layers to create light and shadow patterns visible from the road below. The horizontals of the scrim wall are detailed to create a screen in front of the glass entry vestibule and minimize visibility for onlookers.

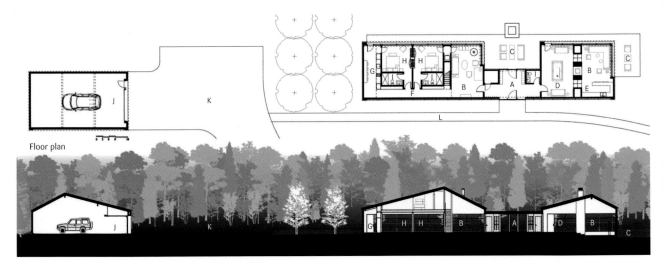

Floor plan

Section

A. Entry
B. Living area
C. Outdoor living area
D. Entertainment area
E. Bar
F. Hall
G. Kitchenette
H. Bedroom
I. Bathroom
J. Garage
K. Driveway
L. Walkway

Site plan

VERNACULAR WOODSHED
AS DESIGN PRECEDENT

VOID
Provide private
views of hillside

ICONIC FORM
Reflect vernacular
landscape

SCRIM WALL
Create engaging surface from
functional element

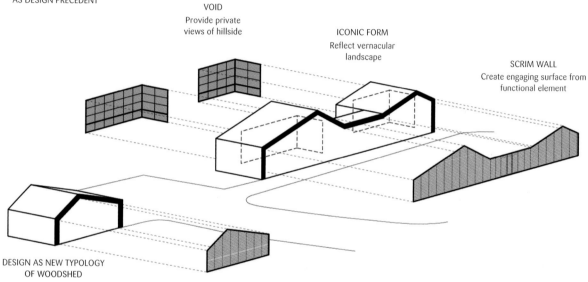

DESIGN AS NEW TYPOLOGY
OF WOODSHED

The western, public elevation of the
cottage presents the continuous, wood
textured wall that evokes the expressive
scrim wall of a traditional woodshed.
The eastern side opens to the woodland
views with a glass facade that invites
the landscape, exterior retaining walls,
and terrace spaces, into the building.

120

The design of rural architecture,
such as cottages and cabins,
often entail the use of passive
solar tactics, which are aimed at
regulating interior temperature with
minimum use of mechanical devices.

Lokal A-frame Cabin is a rehabbed and modernized cabin on 2.5 acres of wooded land fronting the Maurice River. It is Lokal Hotel's first foray into the vacation home rental market, and it brings all of the same high design, boutique hotel amenities that exist in Lokal's flagship hotel in Old City. The founders of Lokal Hotel had been casually searching for the right property, one that was close enough to the city for a quick escape year-round, while also close to the shore for easy beach day trips. Built in the 60s, Lokal A-frame Cabin hadn't been upgraded since, but its bones were great, and the property was just what Lokal's founders were looking for.

Lokal A-frame Cabin
1,500 sq ft

Lokal Hotel
Dochester, New Jersey, United States

© Rocco Avallone and Heidis Bridge

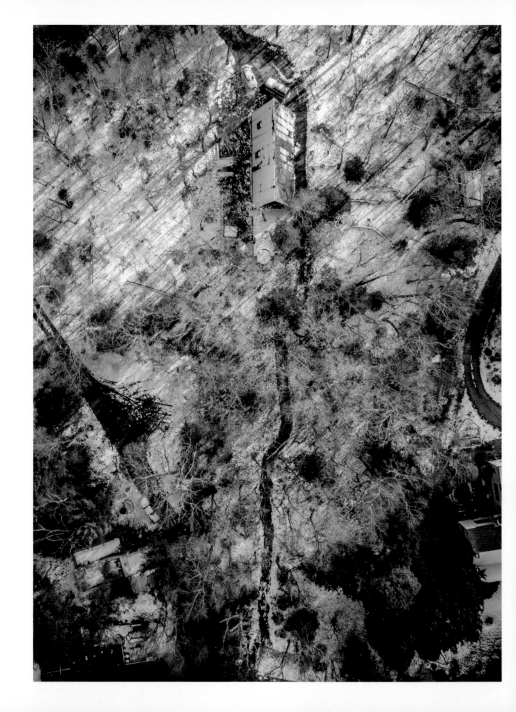

121

Embrace the quiet and peace, the clean air, the energizing hikes in the wilderness, and savor the wonderful moments around a bonfire as the ultimate mountain cabin escape.

While the location and the exterior of the cabin are rustic, the interiors are modern and equipped with contemporary amenities for maximum comfort. The Lokal team chose a Scandinavian aesthetic for the revamped cabin. The material palette consists of concrete, bleached wood flooring, pine plywood paneling, and a combination of matte black and white throughout.

122

The widespread use of plywood paneling can be understood as a contemporary, cost-efficient, and environmentally friendly interpretation of the traditional log cabin.

The cabin contains three bedrooms, two bathrooms, and sleeps up to eight. The first floor contains a bedroom and a full bathroom in addition to the modern living room, kitchen, dining room, and bar. On the upper loft level, there are a queen bedroom and a full bathroom that has a deck overlooking the woods and river.

The atmosphere of the cabin's interior is inviting regardless of the season. Warm and cozy for the cold months of winter, cool and airy during the summer, thanks to a palette of neutral colors.

The basement has been partially
finished into a bunk room with four twin
bed nooks built into the walls and a
small lounge area with a TV.

123

The rustic aesthetic has evolved
into a contemporary design
concept that features rough
textures and warm colors often
associated with nature. It is meant
to provide a relaxed atmosphere
while offering the comfort of a
home away from home.

The Great Lakes Cabin is the first built prototype produced by the Backcountry Hut Company. The cabin is designed to be packaged and shipped to remote locations. The one-story system is based on a ten-foot by sixteen-foot module, but while this modular approach implies architectural functions, opportunities for customization are encouraged. Promoting user participation in the conception, design, and construction of buildings is at the core of The Backcountry Hut Company. The resulting "kit of parts" building system is intended to allow individuals and groups to have more agency in building their structures, and in doing so, ultimately empower people to shape their communities.

Great Lakes Cabin
700 sq ft

Leckie Studio Architecture + Design and The Backcountry Hut Company

Georgian Bay, Ontario, Canada

© James Jones (photography) and Plus Visual (renderings)

124

The compact structure is crafted
to have a minimal environmental
impact on the site.

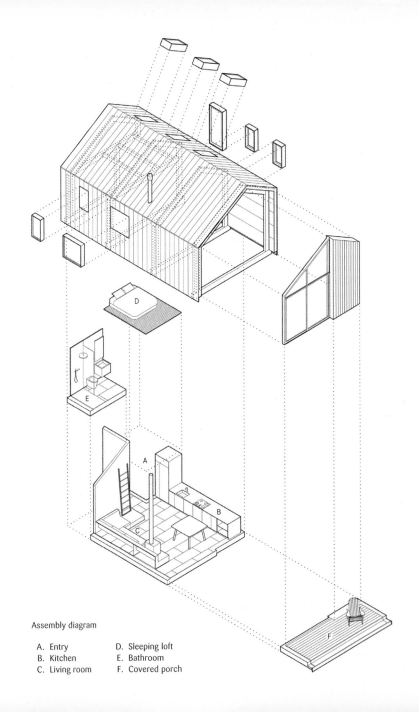

Assembly diagram

A. Entry   D. Sleeping loft
B. Kitchen   E. Bathroom
C. Living room   F. Covered porch

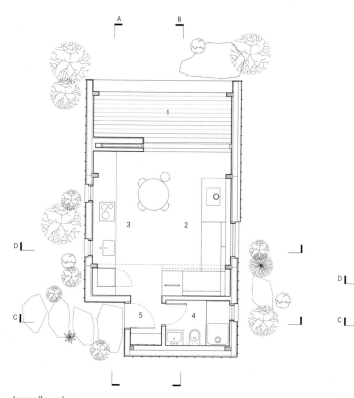

Lower floor plan

1. Porch   5. Entry
2. Living room   6. Bedroom
3. Kitchen   7. Mechanical
4. Bathroom   room

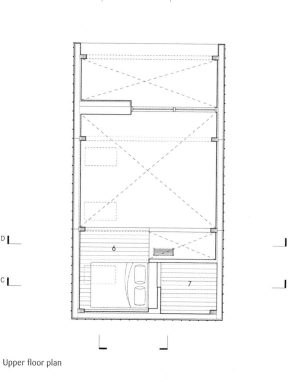

Upper floor plan

The structural system is comprised of a sustainably harvested engineered glulam timber frame, clad with prefabricated insulated wall/roof/floor panels.

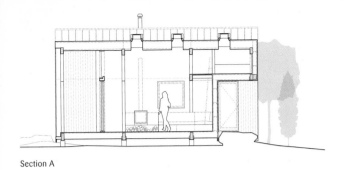

Section A

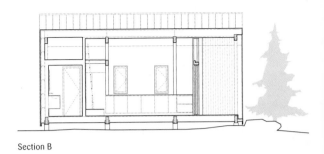

Section B

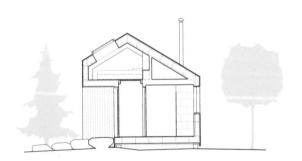

Section C

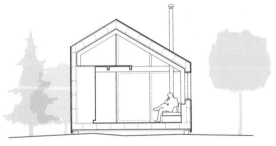

Section D

125

The prefabricated system allows a fast building process of weeks rather than months. The overall process can take between six to twelve months from planning to finish, depending on the complexity of the project.

Every square inch is utilized—featuring a lofted sleeping area, a full bathroom, and covered exterior decks at front and back entries.

Arrowhead Shelter

108 sq ft

**Leckie Studio Architecture +
Design and The Backcountry
Hut Company**

Anywhere in North America

© James Jones (photography)
and Plus Visual (renderings)

The Arrowhead Shelter is a prefabricated structure designed to
be flat-packed and shipped to remote locations across North
America. The A-frame design is, in part, a nostalgic reference to
alpine cabins in the mountains of British Columbia, but it is also
structurally efficient and simple to build by a small group of
people with hand tools. The DIY structures of the Backcountry
Hut Company work to rethink the traditional methods of
architectural practice by directly engaging the fundamental
social, political, cultural, and economic forces that shape the
built environment.

The "kit of parts" system simplifies construction in hard-to-access and remote locations, where the parts arrive flat-packed on pallets.

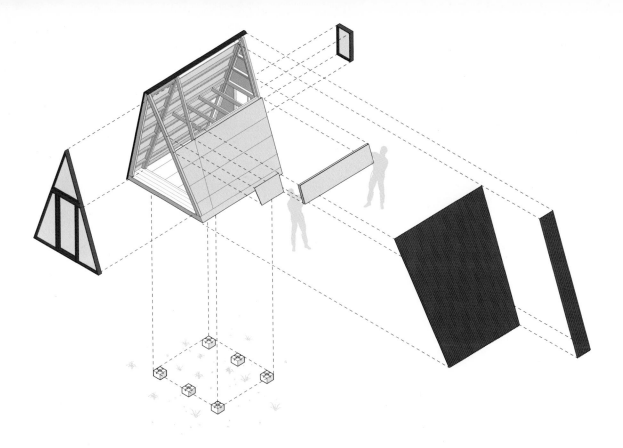

Assembly diagram

126

The prefabricated, mass
customizable building systems
can be configured to meet a wide
range of individual needs.

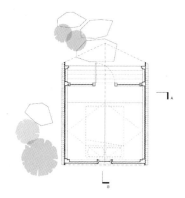

Floor plan

The Arrowhead Shelter design combines the rustic beauty of A-frame building and the sustainable benefits associated with low-cost construction and minimal maintenance.

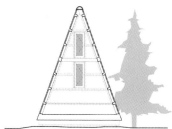

Section A

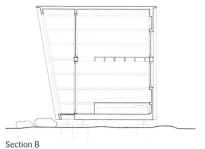

Section B

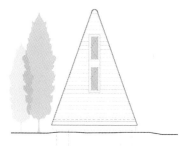

Elevations

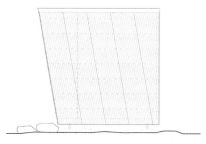

Cabin Ustaoset is situated 3,500 feet above sea level, midway between Oslo and Bergen, at the foot of the mighty Hardangervidda—Europe's highest mountain plateau. With no road connection, construction materials were flown in by helicopter. The groundwork was done carefully, siting the cabin on pillars to preserve as much as possible of the slow-growing vegetation. The exterior of the building had to be finished during the short summer months, while the rest was completed in mid-winter when materials for the interior could be transported in with snow scooters. A preexisting small cabin was maintained. The two structures, facing each other, create a central sheltered outdoor space to enjoy during the good weather.

Cabin Ustaoset
775 sq ft

Jon Danielsen Aarhus
Hol Municipality, Norway
© Knut Bry

127

Roof overhangs protect siding, doors, and windows from water damage.

This modern cabin features floor-to-ceiling windows that showcase the uniform pine cladding on the cabin's exterior and interior.

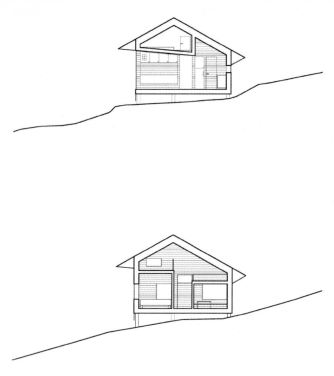

Sections

128

Remoteness suggests serenity and quiet under a star-studded black sky. It offers the opportunity for an ideal getaway to satisfy the need for the full nature experience and authenticity, away from the stressful demands of the urban daily life.

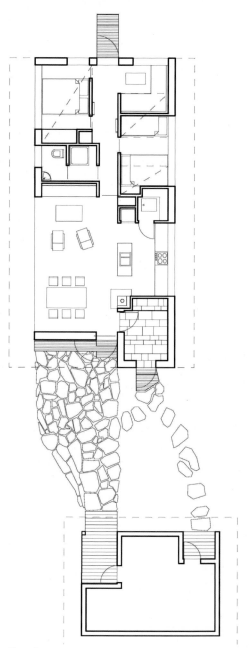

Floor plan

The floor-to-ceiling windows are three-layer, insulating, and solar protected glass panels. They take in the views of the Ustevann Lake, the Hallingskarvet mountains, and the Hardangerjøkulen glacier, providing a sense of being part of this magnificent landscape while maintaining a comfortable temperature inside the cabin.

129

Pine, like other wood types such as spruce, larch, and cedar used for wall cladding, offers excellent insulation and the classic cabin look that one might expect from a mountain retreat.

This house capitalizes on spatial qualities despite its reduced footprint. Built for a family of four, it includes a living room, a kitchen/dining room, a patio, three bedrooms, one bathroom, and two powder rooms. Situated on an elongated plot close to a lake, the positioning of the building is determined by the views of the surrounding natural setting and by sun exposure. With simple yet smart design gestures, the project is of the highest standard, while at the same time implementing energy-efficient and space-saving strategies. In this sense, it's a model example of small home construction: compact and functional without sacrificing design quality in both its interior and its exterior.

Tiny Holiday Home
807 sq ft

i29 interior architects and Chris Collaris

VinKeveen, The Netherlands

© Ewout Huibers

130

The exterior appearance of a
building reflects the programmatic
requirements of its interior and
responds to the qualities of its
surroundings, offering openings
to take in daylight and views, and
solid surfaces to provide shelter
and privacy.

To enhance the sculptural form of the building, the use of materials is kept to a limited selection. Roofing and window detailing are carefully concealed behind the dark wood exterior cladding for a clean look.

North elevation

West elevation

East elevation

South elevation

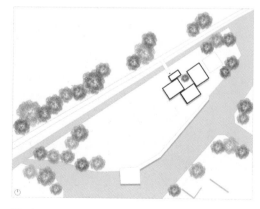

Site plan

131

Fragmenting the massing of buildings brings down their scale to minimize the visual impact and facilitate the integration with their immediate surroundings. This is particularly true in natural settings where construction can be disruptive and, therefore, a more sensible design approach is critical.

132

Visual impact can be minimized by creating a cluster of small attached buildings, instead of a large monolithic structure. This would optimize natural lighting and solar heating and cooling functions.

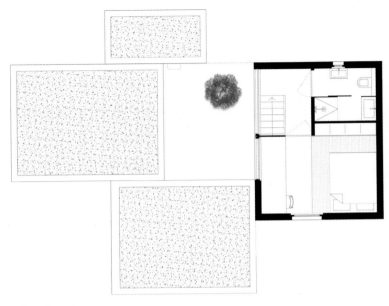

Second floor plan

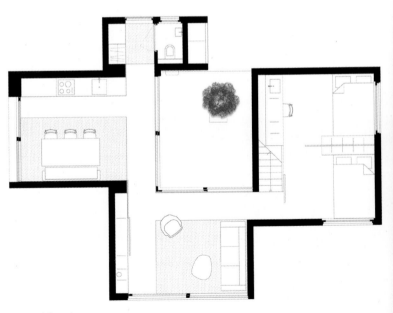

Ground floor plan

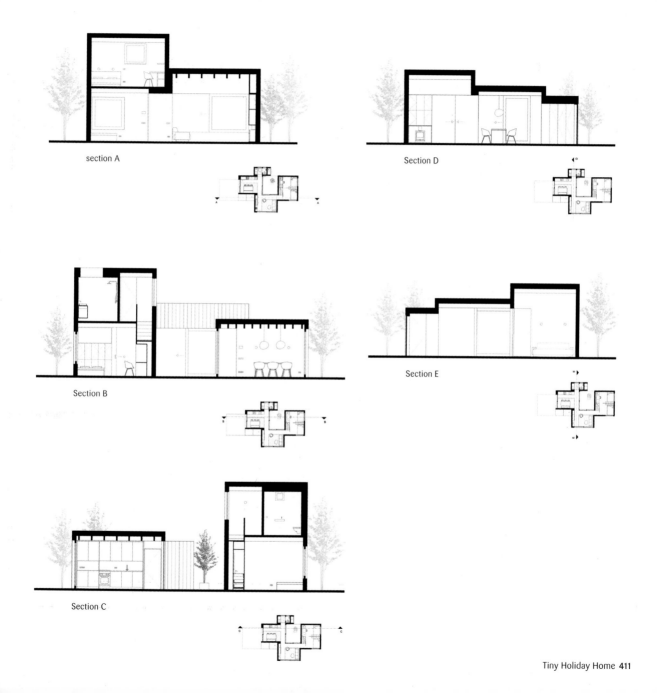

section A

Section B

Section C

Section D

Section E

133

The use of durable and resistant materials and thorough maintenance is necessary to mitigate the potential damage from UV, water, insects, and air infiltration while maintaining the aesthetic appeal of the construction.

Long sightlines across the building's interior provide a sense of amplitude and visual connection between the different areas. This effect is further enhanced with the use of similar finishes both in and out to dissolve the transition between the two realms.

Custom furniture and integrated
cabinetry accentuate the spatial quality
of the home. In every detail, they aimed
for the ultimate space-efficient solution.
Every aspect of the design is approached
to produce a pure and unified experience
and create a strong impression.

134

Built-in cabinetry makes efficient use of limited space, while also providing a cabin with a modern, comfortable look adapted to a contemporary lifestyle.

Lockeport Beach House
2,200 sq ft

Nova Tayona Architects
Nova Scotia, Canada
© Janet Kimber

Within a protected cove along the South Shore of Nova Scotia, time and tides have created a half-mile forested sandbar on which this beach refuge lightly sits. Despite its dramatic location on an expanse of shoreline, the clients were drawn to the internal, cozy character of the site. Scraggly tamarack and spruce trees covered in Old Man's Beard shelter the site from the openness of the beach and create a very specific sense of place. A mandate of protecting the sandbank and the clients' appreciation of hearing the ocean but not seeing it, were starting points for siting strategy. From the beach, and to locals, the house is hidden; its modest siting plays a small role in preserving the unspoiled forest edge and coastline.

The house is elevated on helical piles
bearing twenty feet into the sand,
minimizing excavation, tree clearing,
and sandbank erosion. Oriented
slightly west of south, the design takes
advantage of passive solar orientation,
while catching the light. The deep roof
eave provides shade in the summer and
allows the low winter sun to warm the
concrete floors in the cold season.

The scale and relationship of the private and communal spaces and their views to the exterior reflect the initial impressions of the site—cozy and intimate, yet open and expansive—and express a series of spatial experiences as one moves through the house.

Bright colors reflect light. Dark colors absorb it. These are concepts that have been implemented into passive solar design to turn solar light into a beneficial thermal asset.

Passive solar design takes into account the qualities of a chosen site, the climate, and the building materials to reduce heating and cooling loads through energy-efficiency tactics.

Hillside Sanctuary

4,463 sq ft

Hoedemaker Pfeiffer

San Juan Islands, Washington,
United States

© Kevin Scott

The owner of this property was looking for a personal retreat
inspired by a treasured stone and wood home lost to fire
decades earlier in the hills of Appalachia. The design goal was
not to re-create it but rather to give its spirit new form. Taking
inspiration from its remote site in the San Juan Islands, the
project is a series of simple stone volumes growing naturally
from their rocky surroundings. From that concept emerged a
main cabin and an adjacent annex, each responding to their
own unique location. Together they provide two related but
distinct ways of appreciating the beauty of this site.

The main building is sited on a small plateau high on top of a steeply sloping hillside, taking full advantage of sweeping views. The location suggested a stone plinth and stone wall to form its base and rear elevation. A wood structure perches atop the low stone base creates a nuanced sense of enclosure.

137

The analysis of the geographical and topographical qualities of a site, along with the consideration of the climate, vegetation, and cultural heritage of the area, is the starting point for the design of a site-specific building.

A pair of thick stone walls with fireplaces rising together within the home's interior enhance the concept, separating the main level into public and private realms and flanking a central stone staircase.

The dining room was conceived as a three-sided glass object cantilevering into the tree canopy. Below, a concrete patio offers protected outdoor space. It provides a secondary entry as well as its own distinct view experience.

138

The specific qualities of a site should guide a building design from its siting and orientation through the placement of windows and selection of materials.

The open-plan kitchen, living, and dining areas capitalize on the generous natural lighting and panoramic views while encouraging social interaction and flexible use of the space.

139

Building design must ensure the means of achieving a good indoor climate through the selection of durable and resistant materials and products, including doors and windows, type of glazing, as well as insulating materials.

The cabin and its annex are as much part of the surrounding landscape as the landscape is part of them. This symbiosis is achieved through the use of building materials that blend with the natural surroundings, an orientation that makes the most of the light and views, and the generous fenestration and access to the outdoors.

Casa Caldera is an off-grid retreat located in a remote landscape. The site offers panoramic views of the varied topography, ranging from distant high mountains to wide, open arid plains with low-lying outcroppings. The house emerges from the native grasses, among Emery oaks. Its construction, which takes cues from the vernacular zaguan housing typology, is a simple rectangular form of poured Lavacrete—a mixture of pulverized lightweight red scoria, cement, and water, rammed into the formwork. The material choice responds to the desire to anchor the retreat to the site's geology, while at the same time, offering insulation and thermal mass to ensure indoor comfort.

Casa Caldera

945 sq ft

DUST®

San Rafael Valley, Arizona, United States

© Cade Hayes

The zaguan acts as the connector between the interior and the exterior. Curated apertures cool the home and offer a tight frame for the expansive view, also shifting subtly the quality of light that drifts into the space.

140

Modest architectural designs can promote the integration of manmade structures into their natural settings. Such designs are balanced and pleasantly built environments sensible to the surrounding natural features to connect harmoniously with nature rather than compete with it.

Casa Caldera harnesses the challenges of its remote site, emphasizing sustainable tactics. Cooling is provided by natural cross ventilation through the zaguan and the windows. Water is from a well and solar power is used for minimal electrical needs.

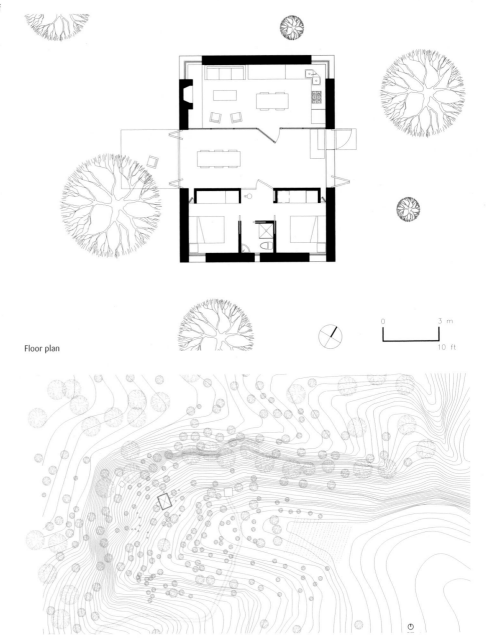

Floor plan

0   3 m

10 ft

Site plan

141

A careful site analysis is necessary from an aesthetic and functional standpoint: It contributes to the optimization of a nature-architecture relationship and the creation of interior layouts that are well adapted to the natural conditions.

142

Site analysis can inform on
the shape and proportions of
interior spaces as well as on the
positioning and sizes of openings
to enhance the relationship
between the built form and nature.

Casa Caldera is designed to be part of
the landscape and make the most of the
environmental qualities of the site. It is
sensible to the surroundings in its scale,
form, and materials while implementing
sustainable strategies to minimize heat
gain and maximize airflow through its
interior spaces.

143

Sensible use of materials and minimal detailing allows the focus on spatial qualities and the surrounding landscape as an integral part of a building composition.

According to the designers, Vipp Shelter is conceived more like a product than a piece of architecture. It is a habitable structure made of black steel and glass that can be placed anywhere. A part of the Vipp Hotel, Vipp Shelter is an invitation to experience the brand's vision to offer unique accommodations in different locations, for experiences out of the ordinary. The hotel is still a small venture with just two rooms, but more are in the making. Vipp Shelter's interior is dark-toned and minimal, allowing focus on what is important: all the nature around.

Vipp Shelter
592 sq ft

Vipp
Lake Immeln, Sweden
© Vipp

Vipp Shelter offers a chance to go
offline and connect with nature with
Immeln Lake at its doorstep and the
deep lush forest all around it.

Vipp Shelter is shaded by the dense tree
canopy. During the winter, when the
trees have lost all of their leaves, the
black surfaces of Vipp Shelter absorb
the heat from the sunlight.

144

Using the principles of passive solar design, the heat accumulated in a thermal mass—walls, floors, and roof—travels to a cooler zone to warm it up.

145

Concrete has good thermal mass, absorbing, storing, and then releasing heat. Its density and conductivity properties make it an excellent construction material to maintain a stable temperature in an interior space.

Skylights bring natural light into interior spaces. While this can be beneficial during the winter months, it can also be a nuisance in the summer. Shading devices are advised to control the amount of light that is let in.

Once inside, Vipp Shelter is more than a habitable steel structure. Lined with tasteful finishes, and fully fitted with contemporary furnishings, appliances, and accessories, Vipp Shelter takes temporary living to a higher level combining domestic comfort, and extraordinary natural setting.

EFC Cabin
1,335 sq ft

VOID

Dota, San Jose, Costa Rica
© Andres Garcia Lachner

The EFC cabin was designed to respond to the cold, foggy climate in the mountains of Dota. It's located on a hill surrounded by a small forest of oak trees. The views, landscape, orientation, wind patterns, and access points were the key factors that guided the design. The cabin, which consists of two differentiated volumes, is built in relationship with its surroundings. One is solid, the other has generous glass walls that allow the living-dining area and the bedrooms to take in the views of the valley, the mountains, and the oak forest. The interior-exterior relationship makes the environment the main element of the cabin harnessing openness and light.

147

A sensible design should respect and work with the established natural features such as the topography, outcroppings, vegetation, and trees, seeking integration between architecture and nature.

148

It is critical that new rural architecture is a positive addition to the chosen site, taking into account the existing natural surroundings to promote a unique sense of place.

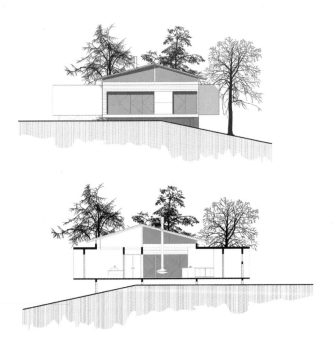

Longitudinal section

Perspective section

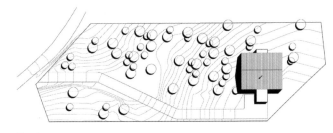

Site plan

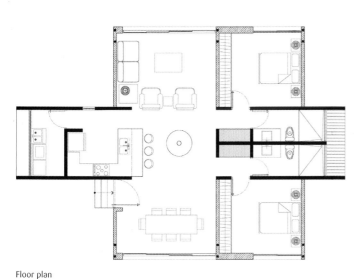

Floor plan

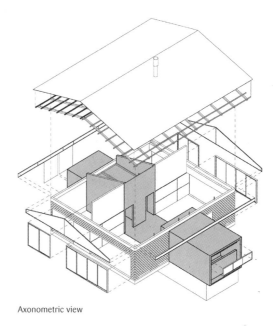

Axonometric view

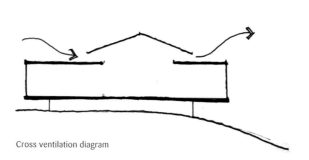

Cross ventilation diagram

The cabin sits lightly on concrete footings among oak trees. It is an architecture that articulates a structure of pine exterior siding and another clad in stone. The interior surfaces are finished in plywood paneling. The two are covered by a corrugated steel roof that appears to float above clerestory windows.

149

The site-specific design approach should reflect the unique character of the place. This can be achieved through the use of locally sourced materials that effortlessly blend with the landscape or with materials that, with time, will weather to merge with the colors and textures of their natural surroundings.

The use of natural materials, such as stone and wood, creates a sense of health and well-being. This sense is linked to the concept of biophilia, which can be defined as humans' innate affinity to nature.

Tunbridge Winter Cabin
1,250 sq ft

New Affiliates

Tunbridge, Vermont,
United States

© Jaffer Kolb and
Michael Vahrenwald/Esto

Sited on a 65-acre property in the Green Mountains of
Vermont, Tunbridge Winter Cabin contains a painting studio
and accommodation for a two-generation family. The structure
is an informal, winter-ready getaway that takes cues from the
traditional Vermont cabin. It is inspired by the area's aggregate
structures, in which barns, houses, and sheds all grow on
and around each other. The impetus was to create an organic
retreat as well as a platform to nurture the creative interests—
including painting, furniture design, and filmmaking—of the
family members.

After the typically informal and loose nature of these vernacular structures, New Affiliates sought to create a design in which regularity is interrupted by slight misalignments and minor asymmetries in the size and placement of architectural details.

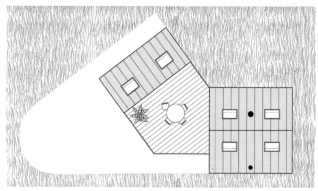

Roof plan

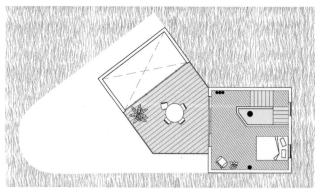

Second floor plan

Diagrams of local aggregate
structures in the area

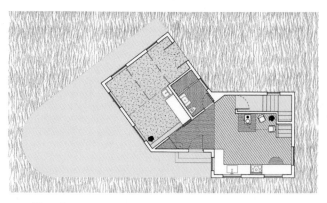

Ground floor plan

The plan consists of two identical squares meeting at a corner, with the triangular space at the hinge serving as the entryway. The double-height studio space comprises one square, and is set off-angle from the living area, which is divided into a single-height first floor space and kitchen, and a second-floor master bedroom with a high-pitched ceiling that opens onto an outdoor deck.

150

Woodburning iron stoves are ideal for spaces ranging from a rustic cabin to a sleek modern home, blending old-time charm and functionality.

Square windows in two sizes frame specific elements of nature, creating a tableau of views that unfold by moving from the studio through the living quarters and spiraling up through the master bedroom to the deck for an ultimately expansive outdoor view.

DIRECTORY

Andrew Michler
Masonville, Colorado, United States
www.hyperlocalarch.com

APPAREIL architecture
Montreal, Quebec, Canada
www.appareilarchitecture.com

Arkitektværelset
Oslo, Norway
www.arkitektvaerelset.no

Atelier BOOM-TOWN
Montreal, Quebec, Canada
www.boom-town.ca

Atelier L'Abri
Montreal, Quebec, Canada
www.labri.ca

AtelierRISTING
Indianapolis, Indiana, United States
www.atelierristing.com

Birdseye Design
Richmond, Vermont, United States
www.birdseyevt.com

Bourgeois / Lechasseur architects
Montreal, Quebec, Canada
www.bourgeoislechasseur.com

Cardin Julien
Montreal, Quebec, Canada
www.cardinjulien.com

Coates Design Architects
Bainbridge Island, Washington,
United States
www.coatesdesign.com

Copeland Associates Architects
Auckland, New Zealand
www.copelandassociates.co.nz

Cohesion by Malek Alqadi
Los Angeles, California, United States
www.thecohesionstudio.com

D U S T®
Tucson, Arizona, United States
www.dustdb.com

Framestudio
Oakland, California, United States
www.framedesign.studio

Gonzalo Iturriaga Arquitectos
Vitacura, Santiago Province, Chile
www.gonzaloiturriaga.cl

GreenSpur
Falls Church, Virginia, United States
www.greenspur.net

Hoedemaker Pfeiffer
Seattle, Washington, United States
www.hoedemakerpfeiffer.com

Hyperlocal Workshop
Masonville, Colorado, United States
www.hyperlocalarch.com

i29 architects
Ouder-Amstel, The Netherlands
www. i29.nl

Jean Verville Architecte
Montreal, Quebec, Canada
www.jeanverville.com

Jon Danielsen Aarhus
Oslo, Norway
www.jdaa.no

Kariouk Associates
Ottawa, Ontario, Canada
www.kariouk.com

LAMZ Arquitectura
Oaxaca, Mexico
www.lamzarquitectura.com

Lazor / Office Design
Minneapolis, Minnesota, United States
www.lazoroffice.com

Leckie Studio Architecture + Design
Vancouver, British Columbia, Canada
www.leckiestudio.com

Liberté Tiny Houses
Werkendam, The Netherlands
www.libertetinyhouses.nl

Lokal Hotel
Philadelphia, Pennsylvania, United States
www.staylokal.com

Lund+Slaatto Architects
Oslo, Norway
www.lsa.no

MSR Architects
Minneapolis, Minnesota, United States
www.msrdesign.com

Midland Architecture
Pittsburg, Pennsylvania and Columbus,
Ohio; United States
www.midlandarch.com

Moxon Architects
London, England and Aberdeenshire,
Scotland; United Kingdom
www.moxonarchitects.com

New Affiliates
New York, New York, United States
www.new-affiliates.us

Nova Tayona Architects
Toronto, Ontario, Canada
www.novatayonaarchitects.com

Paul Cashin Architects
Hampshire, United Kingdom
www.paulcashinarchitects.co.uk

Prentiss + Balance + Wickline
Seattle and Winthrop, Washington,
United States
www.pbwarchitects.com

Salmela Architects
Duluth, Minnesota, United States
www.salmelaarchitect.com

Sanden + Hodnekvam
Nesoddtangen, Norway
www.sandenhodnekvam.no

Sean O'Neill
Seattle, Washington, United States
www.seanoneill.us

Stinessen Arkitektur
Tromsø, Norway
www.snorrestinessen.com

studio 3A
Lisbon, Portugal
www.studio-3a.com

Superkül
Toronto, Ontario, Canada
www.superkul.ca

The Backcountry Hut Company
Vancouver, British Columbia, Canada
www.thebackcountryhutcompany.com

The Way We Build
Amsterdam, The Netherlands
www.thewaywebuild.com

Vipp
Copenhagen, Denmark
www.vipp.com

VOID
San Jose, Costa Rica
www.voidcr.com

Y100 ateliér
Banská Bystrica, Slovakia
www.y100.sk

yh2 architecture
Montreal, Quebec, Canada
www.yh2architecture.com